D0982921

EASTERN EUROPE
AND THE COLD WAR
PERCEPTIONS AND PERSPECTIVES

Stephen Fischer-Galati

EAST EUROPEAN MONGRAPHS, BOULDER
DISTRIBUTED BY COLUMBIA UNIVERSITY PRESS, NEW YORK
1994

EAST EUROPEAN MONOGRAPHS, NO. CD

Copyright 1994 by Stephen Fischer-Galati
ISBN 0-88033-297-2
Library of Congress Catalog Card Number 94-61564

Printed in the United States of America

FOR ANNE, WENDY, AND NANCY
Who taught me everything

CONTENTS

FORWARD

It would seem presumptuous for the editor of the East European Monographs to publish a collection of his own papers on a topic that may be regarded as "*déjà vu* all over again." However, the evolution of Eastern Europe during the five years following the official end of the Cold War seems to justify a few reflections on the historic place of Eastern Europe in the years of confrontation between the United States and the Soviet Union that are still known as the period of the Cold War.

It is not necessary to rehash the conflicting theories on the origins of the Cold War, nor is it to review the controversies regarding the motivations of the two protagonists in the conflict. Suffice it to say, for our purposes, that Stalin's takeover of Eastern Europe was not motivated by a desire to liberate the member nations of the so-called Soviet Bloc from social, economic, and political oppression identified with the "lackeys of Anglo-American imperialism" and that the liberation of Eastern Europe from communism through a "crusade for freedom" that would lift the "Iron Curtain" was not the paramount factor in Truman's decision to oppose Soviet imperialism. What is certain, however, is that control over Eastern Europe was deemed vital by the Kremlin during most of the duration of the Cold War while *de facto* recognition of Soviet hegemony over member nations of its bloc by the United States became evident in the age of peaceful coexistence of the 1950s and beyond.

Under these circumstances, American - and to a lesser degree, Western - interests in, and concern with, Eastern Europe was essentially limited to paying lip service to the "restoration of democracy," to denouncing Soviet aggression in Hungary in 1956 and Czechoslovakia in 1968, to seeking protection of human rights and, above all, to encouraging "independent" or "separate" roads to, or forms of, socialism such as the Yugoslav, Romanian, and later Hungarian and Czechoslovak on the assumption that such manifestations would weaken the cohesion of the Soviet Bloc, if not necessarily lead to democracy or the collapse of the Soviet empire.

The effectiveness of American policies and actions designed to encourage "socialism with a human face" and "national" leaderships within Eastern Europe, while concurrently supporting émigré political and intellectual leaders and organizations ostensibly committed to democracy, is difficult to ascertain. It is evident that the collapse of communism in Eastern Europe was organically related to the collapse of the Soviet Union;

it is less evident, however, that the collapse of communism throughout Eastern Europe and the Soviet Union was due to an American victory in the Cold War or, in the case of Eastern Europe as such, to American policies that allowed the national democratic forces to overcome the forces of communist oppression.

The present volume is designed to assess the place of Eastern Europe during the Cold War period in the broader perspective of the historic evolution of Eastern Europe in the nineteenth and twentieth centuries. This approach seems justifiable in that historic legitimacy has been a prerequisite for power, an integral component of political and popular culture, and a dominant element in resistance to illegitimate foreign oppressors. The Soviet domination of Eastern Europe *per se* was not an historic aberration, but communism in its Stalinist and neo-Stalinist forms was. However, as authoritarianism, religious and secular paternalism, and Christian populism were in keeping with the historic evolution and political and popular cultures, democracy was not necessarily a prerequisite for liberation from communist oppression. And these realities, evident before the Cold War, survived - albeit muted during the communist period itself - and are resurfacing in the 1990s.

It may be argued that the historic perspective is not the best way to evaluate the place of Eastern Europe in the Cold War in that it tends to be unscientific and subjective. This may indeed be so. But the reconstruction of the history of Eastern Europe during the period of the Cold War through a collection of articles written at various times and at various stages of the evolution of the last century also entails the author's perception of the significance of events and developments. In this instance, that perception is based on first-hand familiarity with pre-communist Eastern Europe and on understanding the realities of the communist and post-communist periods derived from unique opportunities afforded to me during the last thirty years.

It is fair to say that as the editor of the *East European Quarterly* and of the *East European Monographs*, as a participant at endless conferences and as a lecturer on East European history and civilization, I have known an unusually large number of colleagues and students in and from Eastern Europe. However, I have also had the opportunity to travel extensively in the East European countryside, to meet with people from other walks of life, to listen to the street, to gain a sense of the concerns, mentalities, and expectations of various segments of the population.

I would be derelict if I were to emulate recipients of awards and other "name-droppers" in acknowledging the assistance given to me in the pursuit of work on Eastern Europe. But I would also be derelict if I would fail to acknowledge the assistance given by those who, over the years, have opened "windows of opportunity" for gathering knowledge not readily accessible to outsiders during the Cold War era. In chronological order, I express my gratitude to Andrew Gyorgy, James Clarke, R. V. Burks, Alfred Kelly, Frederick Praeger, Constantin Daicoviciu, Emil Condurachi, Eugen Stanescu, George Minden, Mihai Berza, Basil and Louise Laoudras, Trixi and her friends, William Crawford, Dimitrije Djordjevic, Walter Leitsch, Peter Hanak, William Griffith, Georges Castellan, Ludovit Holotik, Corneliu Bogdan, Béla Kiraly, Lawson Crowe, Robert Tilley, Joseph Held, Constantin and Dinu Giurescu, the Center for Military History - Bucharest, Kate Wittenberg, John Bradley, Agustin Buzura and his associates, Ioan Donca, and Lia Ciplea.

Boulder, Colorado
August, 1994

CHAPTER ONE

EASTERN EUROPE IN THE TWENTIETH CENTURY: "OLD WINE IN NEW BOTTLES"

Three times during the twentieth century - in 1918, 1945, and 1989 - Eastern Europe was to be made "safe for democracy." The dismantling of the empires of the Habsburgs, Ottoman sultans, Russian tsars, Hitler's Germany, and that of the Soviet Union in the face of the irresistible force of the oppressed nations' quest for democracy has fulfilled the axiomatic ideological position of Western champions of the principle of self-determination of nationalities. Yet even after the overthrow of the most pernicious forms of totalitarianism democracy remains illusory. It may well be asked what factors mitigated against the triumph of democracy after the world wars and to what extent these factors remain relevant today.

The failure of democracy to take root or to develop in the way that Woodrow Wilson, Franklin Delano Roosevelt, and others expected has been attributed, in rather simplistic terms, to a variety of external and internal developments that are presumably becoming irrelevant. The rise of totalitarianism in Italy, Germany, and the Soviet Union in the interwar years taken in conjunction with French and British appeasement and American isolationism, as well as the economic devastation caused by the Great Depression, had a negative impact on the democratic evolution of Eastern Europe. Similarly, Western errors at Yalta, reflecting political naïveté with respect to Stalin's aggressive imperialism, made possible the conquest of Eastern Europe by the Soviet Union. According to the proponents of such explanations, the forces of democracy that have prevailed in Germany since World War II are making headway in the Soviet Union itself under Mikhail Gorbachev. These forces are being supplemented and reinforced by Japan, the United States, and a European community vocally committed to the promotion of human rights, tolerance of ethnic and religious diversity, political pluralism, a market economy, and a new world order. These factors are likely to further and facilitate the democratic revolution and evolution of Eastern Europe in the future.

Internal factors, designed to explain the retardation of the democratic evolution of the nations of Eastern Europe, range over a wide area. They include the standard lack of democratic experience in the face of fascist aggression in the 1930s and the more realistic assessment of nationalist excesses and internecine conflicts between diverse ethnic, nationalistic, and religious groups. In addition, we must consider the failure of ruling elites to address social and economic inequities, with a corresponding exacerbation of class conflicts leading to the eventual failure of fledgling democratic experiments of the interwar period. Western analysts routinely attribute the inability of democratic forces to assert themselves after World War II to Stalinism and neo-Stalinism. However, with the removal of the barriers to democracy following the collapse of the communist regimes of Eastern Europe in 1989, the democratic inclinations of the peoples of Eastern Europe, inflamed by decades of totalitarian repression, are assumed to have been unleashed and to be bound to triumph in the age of *perestroika* and *glasnost*.

As appealing as these premises may be for interested parties and well-wishers, it may be well worth assessing their validity in the light of the historic realities of the twentieth century. It is indisputable that external factors played a major role in the destablization of Eastern Europe in the interwar years, yet the failure of the democratic experiments might more reasonably be attributed primarily to internal factors in all the Eastern bloc countries (except perhaps Czechoslovakia).

The presumption that the principle of self-determination of nationalities represented the ultimate expression of the oppressed nations' search for and commitment to Wilsonian democracy and peaceful coexistence among the peoples of Eastern Europe on both intra- and international bases was erroneous from its inception. It simply ignored prevailing political, cultural, and socioeconomic realities. By the end of World War I, social, economic, and political retardation were characteristic of most of the region. The largely agrarian, semi-literate societies were politically immature; they were certainly uncommitted to - and in most cases, unfamiliar with - democracy. The political culture, such as it was, had its roots in ecclesiastical and monarchical paternalism. This was most evident in the Orthodox and Catholic communities which comprised the majority of the inhabitants of the successor states. State armies, with their inherent stratifications that cut across some nationalist, religious, and class lines, provided points of identification, but little in the way of political organization. It seems fair to surmise that church, monarchy, and army were no more committed to Wilsonian democracy than were the majority of political organizations striving for leadership in the struggle for national independence and self-determination. National self-determination presupposed the total elimination of the imperial orders and the creation of the largest national states from the remnants of empires and competing national states. Nationalism, often virulent, became the standard for all political groups seeking the support of the masses and the ear of the peace-makers committed to the dissolution of the empires and creation of democratic states. This brand of nationalism, however, was generally intolerant of religious and ethnic diversity and focused most explicitly on territorial issues. Disputes over the borders of the successor states tended to exacerbate conflicts among various ethnic and religious groups. In this respect most inflammatory was the singling out of Jews - outcasts both on religious and ethnic grounds - as not only unidentifiable with national causes but also as overt opponents of national states by virtue of their presumed affiliation with Bolshevism.

The extent of political negativism and intolerance varied from country to country. It was least evident in urbanized and industrialized Bohemia and Moravia in present day Czechoslovakia. It was most striking in Hungary and Romania, albeit for different reasons. The Hungarians resented the loss of Transylvania to Romania more than any other territorial loss they suffered at the end of World War I. The revolution that brought to power the communist regime of Béla Kun contained the roots of an identification of Hungarian Jews with Bolshevism. In turn, the leaders of Greater Romania fearful of Hungarian irredentism and, even more so, of the Bolsheviks' rejection of the annexation of Bessarabia by Romania in 1918, made the defense of the country's national and territorial integrity against Hungarians and "Judeo-Communists" a sine qua non for political success.

This is not to say that the masses of Eastern Europe were swayed by such political arguments or that they were committed to nationalist doctrine. Nor can it be said that all political organizations rejected democratic principles. In a few instances, they even attempted to establish truly democratic political institutions and practices. However, the traditional conservative forces - church, monarchy, and army - favored and supported nationalist, anti-communist, anti-Semitic, and essentially nondemocratic and antidemocratic organizations that, at least in the 1920s, were willing to support the traditional pillars of the political culture of their underdeveloped societies.

The political dynamics of the successor states were relatively simple. In the absence of historical models of pluralism and representative government, the various political parties founded at the beginning of the century and, with increasing frequency, after World War I, did not necessarily command the confidence of their constituents. Conservative as well as liberal political organizations, often headed by the landed gentry, urban businessmen, industrialists, and intellectuals, generally failed to gain the allegiance of the masses. The socialist and social-democratic organizations, which functioned primarily in Czechoslovakia and Hungary, and, to a lesser extent, in Romania and Poland, were vulnerable because of their popular identification with communist and Jewish influences.

The principal target in most of Eastern Europe was the peasant, not because most politicians identified with rural society and its interests or, for that matter, were of peasant origin themselves, but rather because the key socioeconomic issues of the successor states revolved around the redistribution of land and attendant problems. Land reform, redistribution of wealth, industrialization, urbanization, social dislocation, and modernization in general all involved, in one way or another, the peasantry. The peasant concerns were most acute in Romania, Bulgaria, Hungary, and Poland and, to a lesser degree, in certain parts of Yugoslavia and Czechoslovakia. Peasant parties by a variety of names - Agrarian, Smallholder, National Peasant - all championed vaguely defined interests of the rural masses: more often than not, however, ineffectually and for the benefit of the leadership. With the most notable exception of the Bulgarian Agrarian party, headed by Alexander Stamboliiski, the peasant parties failed to meet the expectations of their constituents, which were ultimately grounded in the unhindered possession and exploitation of the land. The radicalism of Stamboliiski's reforms and securing of political power for the peasants' benefit revealed the peasantry's great intolerance toward urban society and governmental bureaucracies. It also revealed the peasants' distinctly anti-intellectual, parochial, antimodern, and antinational attitudes. All this scared not only the conservative elites but also liberals, socialists, communists, and even many of the leaders of Eastern European agrarian organizations. These in general favored compromises that would assure economic progress for the peasantry while subordinating the peasants' interests to those of urban politicians, businessmen, industrialists, and intellectuals.

Political activity, therefore, focused initially on the adaptation of underdeveloped agrarian societies to the social and economic problems of the interwar years. But land reforms were usually insufficiently generous to provide a base for a profitable agricultural economy and industrialization. With few exceptions, these economies were slow and not competitive in European markets. Thus the economic viability of most of the successor states soon became questionable. Instead of seeking meaningful solutions to their countries' economic and related social problems, political parties tended to direct their activities at narrow confrontational issues mostly concerned with ethnic and religious diversity, communism, territorial revisionism, nepotism, and corruption. By the end of the 1920s the democratic structures mandated by the victorious Allies at the end of World War I had been seriously compromised in Poland, Albania, Bulgaria, and Yugoslavia (where de facto dictatorships were in place), were limping along in Hungary, and showed signs of discomfiture in Romania. Czechoslovakia alone, by virtue of its successful urban and industrial traditions and policies, was true to its commitment to pluralistic, parliamentary democracy.

What is noteworthy is this diminution, if not outright failure, of the democratic experiment is that it occurred at a time of relative international peace and prosperity. Indeed, in the 1920s none of the later revisionist or aggressive European powers or their client states posed serious threats to the beneficiaries of the territorial awards made at the end of World War I. The Russo-Polish war ended in Poland's favor; Russian revisionism could be ignored also by Romania; and Mussolini's attempted subversion of Yugoslavia's territorial and political integrity was largely ineffectual. Hungarian irredentism, in the absence of external support, posed no threat to Romania, Yugoslavia, or Czechoslovakia, while Bulgarian agitation over Macedonia and the Dobrudja caused little alarm in Yugoslavia and Romania. Nevertheless, such revisionist activities could be - and were - used to foment xenophobic agitation by political organizations and ruling elites seeking legitimacy and/or the furthering of their political standing within various segments of the respective populations. This was true equally of winners and losers. The fact remains, however, that international issues and territorial disputes were only marginally responsible for the waning of democracy on the eve of the crises of the 1930s.

The political turmoil in Romania, for instance, erupted from the challenge of the moderate National Peasant party to the authoritarian and virtually monopolistic hold on power by the National Liberal party as well as from the gradual evolution of the populist, anti-Semitic, and protofascist Legion of the Archangel Michael. In Hungary, the consolidation of power by Admiral Horthy's authoritarian regime was realized through legitimation of resistance to communism, following the fall of Béla Kun's communist republic, and through invoking the need for a strong regime to secure the historic territorial rights of the Hungarians. In Yugoslavia the political crisis centered on the challenge to Serbian power by Croatia. In Bulgaria the army and urban establishment assumed power after Stamboliiski's assassination in the name of protecting the national interest against subversion by the communists on the left and by the extremist Internal Macedonian Revolutionary Organization (IMRO) on the right. For similar reasons, related to political instability caused by interparty conflicts and perceived threats to Polish integrity, General Joseph Pilsudski established his dictatorship, following a coup d'état, in 1926. Finally, political restiveness in tribal Albania, provoked largely by left-wing intellectuals in confrontation with ultraconservative landowners, made short shrift of democratic procedures as Ahmed Bey Zog established a de fact dictatorship in 1925.

In the absence of solid foundations for the establishment of the practice of Western-style democracy, given the general acceptance by the population and conservative pillars of society of authoritarian rule, the few truly democratic forces in Eastern Europe were fighting a losing battle against the impact of the Great Depression and the corollary rise of the aggressive totalitarianism of the right in the 1930s.

Yet it would be difficult to account for the gradual demise of democracy in the decade before World War II only in terms of economic adversity and external subversion by Mussolini's Italy and Hitler's Germany. The economic crisis of the 1930s affected underdeveloped Eastern Europe much less dramatically than the industrial West. It is true that the economies were generally stagnant, but the internal political crises were largely unrelated to economic factors. The assassination of King Alexander of Yugoslavia by extremists belonging to the IMRO in 1934, for instance, had little to do with economics. For that matter, the subsequent intensification of internecine conflicts (most notably the Serbian-Croatian one) was only marginally connected with the deterioration of the Yugoslav economy. Nor can it be argued that the extraordinary rise to power of the virulently anti-Semitic Romanian Iron Guard was due to mass resentment over alleged economic exploitation of the Romanian worker and peasant by Jewish entrepreneurs. The assumption of power in Poland by the "colonels" was unrelated to the economic woes of the impoverished Polish peasantry. The political turmoil of the 1930s can be better explained by Italian and German interference in the internal affairs of the successor states. The fascists' and Nazis' influence exacerbated internal and international frictions and conflicts and eventually subverted all political orders and activities within Eastern Europe.

Mussolini's support of the IMRO and of Bulgarian irredentism toward Yugoslavia clearly destabilized Alexander's royal dictatorship. Also, Italian support of Croatian separatism, which became reality in 1939, undermined the precarious stability of the authoritarian regency headed by Alexander's cousin, Prince Paul, and facilitated the eventual dissolution of the entire kingdom. However, even without Mussolini's work, the Serbo-Croatian confrontation was reaching the crisis stage by the mid-1930s, propelled, on the one hand, by Catholic Croatian leaders and, on the other, by the Serbian political establishment, both engaged in a struggle for political power within Yugoslavia. It would be fair to say that neither protagonist was thinking in terms of democratic alternatives, compromises, and solutions. Moreover, when Nazi Germany destroyed Yugoslavia after crushing Serbian resistance in 1941, it should be remembered that the Serbs fought the Germans not for the preservation of democracy but in defense of the Serbian nation.

Nor was Mussolini's influence of paramount importance in strengthening Horthy's authoritarianism in Hungary. Fascist Italy did support Hungarian irredentism, in part to undermine the antirevisionist Little Entente of Yugoslavia, Czechoslovakia, and Romania. But the movement to the right in Hungary, manifested in its extremist form by the actions of the xenophobic and anti-Semitic Arrow Cross movement, was closely related to the antiurbanism and anti-intellectualism of the proletariat, peasantry, and clergy all united against Jewish enclaves in Budapest and other urban centers. Mussolini's influence was evident in Poland, yet the homespun military rule of the colonels was based on the traditional invocation of the threat posed to the Polish nation by German and Russian imperialism and by Jewish economic power and influence.

Mussolini's activities are generally agreed to have been less pernicious and significant in affecting the history of pre-World War II Eastern Europe than Hitler's. It is incontestable that Nazi Germany's moves against Poland (starting with the Danzig crisis) and against Czechoslovakia (first via the Sudetenland), when combined with economic penetration and extension of support to extremist organizations, threatened political stability and encouraged antidemocratic forces throughout Eastern Europe. But Hitler exploited, rather than created, conditions favorable for the destabilization of political systems. The nationality question in Czechoslovakia, for instance, was not as relaxed as suggested by contemporary and later champions of the merits of Czechoslovak democracy. The Sudeten Germans' resentment over the monopoly of power enjoyed by Prague largely accounted for their susceptibility to German revisionist propaganda. The Slovaks, strongly Catholic and subject to clerical influence, were jealous of Czech economic and political power and Prague's apparent disdain for the country's "second-class" Slovak citizens. It is not that they were pro-Hitler, but rather that certain elements of fascist doctrine and practices were acceptable to and, in some cases, embraced by the Slovak political leadership. In fact, "clerico-fascism," which became so overt later in Slovakia, had its roots in the political culture of interwar Czechoslovakia. What was true of clerico-fascism in Slovakia was also true in Catholic Croatia and Slovenia and, more than anywhere else, in the Romanian Iron Guard's legionary movement.

The Iron Guardist movement was the ultimate expression of unbridled nationalism, populism, and anti-Semitism in Eastern Europe. The movement paralleled Nazism in its origins and development, differing mainly in terms of the political culture and societal structures of the countries in which it flourished. As a product of traditional Romanian nationalism and anti-Semitism adapted to post-World War I conditions, it was an expression of the rejection by young men and women, mostly of peasant origin, of modernization. Identifying all the evils of modernization with Jewish or pro-Jewish values and ideologies, the "legionnaires of the Archangel Michael," with the blessing of much of the clergy, preached a variant of Christian populism that sought the extirpation of Judeo-communist influences and a return to neo-medieval "Autocracy, Orthodoxy, Nationality." It is important to recognize, however, that the Iron Guard had little, if any, direct financial and only limited political support from Nazi Germany.

There is thus insufficient merit in the theory that the crises and de facto abandonment of democratic rule in Eastern Europe prior to the *Anschluss* of March 1938 were ascribable primarily to external factors. Rather, the factors that accounted for the decline and later abandonment of democratic practices were primarily of internal origin, related as they were to confrontational situations involving immature political organizations tending to encourage and exploit prejudices held by the politically immature masses. Most of the political parties of Eastern Europe were essentially forged in defiance of a group or regime rather than evolving from positive common aims, such as reform, change, or adaptation to conditions that could have promoted economic viability, resolution of social problems, modernization, democratization, international reconciliation, and toleration of diversity. In the absence of positive programs and solutions, conservative, antidemocratic, nationalistic forces at the grassroot and governmental levels steered the internal forces of the countries of Eastern Europe, with the partial exception of Czechoslovakia, toward a generally stagnant course.

External factors became decisive after the annexation of Austria by Hitler and the ensuing Nazi moves to dismember Czechoslovakia. The growing evidence of French and British abandonment of Eastern Europe combined with the rekindling of Stalin's interest in preventing the expansionist moves of the Axis powers into Russia's own *cordon sanitaire* made meaningful democratic opposition to authoritarian rule - ostensibly designed to safeguard national interests against foreign and domestic threats - virtually impossible. Instead, even before the absorption of Czechoslovakia in 1939, the struggle for power in Eastern Europe involved, both internally and internationally, confrontations between radical and moderate antidemocratic forces all jockeying for support from Hitler and/or Mussolini. The irredentism of Poland and Hungary, for instance, with respect to what was left of Czechoslovakia, of Hungary and Bulgaria to what was left of Romania following the Soviet seizure of Bessarabia and northern Bukovina in early 1940, was indicative not only of the mentalities and modus operandi of the leaders but also of the significance of virulent nationalism as a determinant of political attitudes. The bloody confrontations between Romanians and Hungarians following the partitioning of Transylvania in 1940, the mutual extermination of Serbs and Croats in partitioned Yugoslavia, and the brutal treatment of Jews in Romania, Poland, and Slovakia were not ordered by Nazi Germany or Fascist Italy; rather, they were initiated or approved by those nations' rulers themselves with the consent of most of their subjects.

Militant nationalism determined the actions of Eastern Europe in World War II. Romania voluntarily joined Nazi Germany in the war against the Soviet Union for liberation of the territories seized by Stalin in 1940, for the incorporation of Transnistria, populated by people of Romanian origin, and for the destruction of Judeo-communism. Hungary, which had joined the Axis before Romania to further its territorial claims against its neighbors, also fought against the Soviet Union. Bulgaria secured the support of the Axis for its territorial demands and joined it formally, however, without participating in the war against the Soviet

Union. Anti-Czech and anti-Semitic sentiments characterized Slovakia's pro-Nazi regime, led by Bishop Hlinka.

Nationalism was also a source of opposition to Nazi Germany in Poland (which also opposed the Soviet Union) and parts of occupied Yugoslavia. Still, nationalists seldom were committed to reconciliation of ethnic or religious divisions. It should be noted that even those who opposed the occupying forces and native dictatorial regimes held out few prospects for democracy. That was true of Mihailović's Cetniks and Tito's Partisans, of the small Eastern European communist or procommunist underground, and even of the anti-communist and anti-Nazi Polish freedom fighters who could not resolve their differences on the political organization of a restored postwar Poland. Moreover, even when the defeat of Nazi Germany became imminent and the formulation of postwar political patterns could be entertained, the predominant issues were still related to territorial matters. The only democratic solutions to the problems of Eastern Europe toward the end of the war were propounded by the Czech and Polish governments-in-exile and by a handful of political leaders in areas "liberated" by the Soviet armed forces. Their views and legitimacy were, however, unacceptable to the Soviet Union and given only token support by the Western Allies. The aims of this tiny minority were also questioned by at least some of their own compatriots.

The defeat of Hitler, while clearly welcomed by the vast majority of the peoples of Eastern Europe, was not a source of jubilation, since the alternative of communist rule enforced by Stalin's armies and agents was dreaded by most of the politically-conscious elements of the population. Few pinned their hopes on the Western Allies' supporting democratic alternatives despite the rhetoric of Washington and London. Under the circumstances, the political leadership representing organizations that had been active in the interwar years and had not cooperated with the Nazis or native dictatorships thought primarily in terms of accommodation with the communists and leftist groups supported or tolerated by Moscow rather than of championing Western democracy. Only the naive or the foolhardy were willing to assume great risks in the forlorn hope of meaningful American, or even British, support. As collaboration with the communists became essential for survival, issues related to the democratization of the political and social order in a manner contrary to communist plans for modernization on Stalinist patterns were all but forgotten and the very meaning of democracy was altered. By 1947 "people's democracy," a euphemism for communism, had for all intents and purposes replaced "bourgeois democracy," by then a euphemism for fascism and other varieties of anti-communism embodied by the capitalist West.

The evolution of political attitudes after the end of World War II remains unclear. There are no blanket answers because, in fact, not everyone had been against right-wing authoritarianism or against communism or, for that matter, in favor of democratic alternatives. There was no overriding desire among the peoples to bring war criminals to justice or for reconciliation of outstanding ethnic or religious differences, for toleration of diversity, for market economies, for restoration of multi-party systems. Even in Yugoslavia, which was "liberated from fascism" by Tito's Partisans rather than by the Soviet armies, enthusiasm for "Yugoslavism" was limited. Serbian nationalists forgave neither the destruction of the Cetniks nor the atrocities committed by the Croatian Ustaši. However, Tito's opposition to Stalinist imperialism made Yugoslavism a principal element of Titoism and, as such, at least palatable to the inhabitants of the country.

Elsewhere in Eastern Europe, where Soviet armies were present and Stalin's agents active, the masses reacted according to their own political experience. For example, in Romania, with a small industrial working class and a large peasantry, the communists and their allies had little support. Whatever following they enjoyed was the result of land reform and the restitution of northern Transylvania, on Stalin's dictate, to Romania. However, the predominance of Jews and Hungarians in the communist movement and the presence of Russian forces in the country revived nationalism and anti-Semitism to war-time levels. In Hungary, the loss of part of Transylvania together with Jewish visibility in the communist movement made support for the communists scarce and exacerbated the traditional anti-Semitism and anti-Romanianism of the population. In Poland, the communists who had been associated with resistance to the Nazis during the war were initially identified with Polish national interests and, as such, had popular support as nationalists. Anti-communism became significant only after the communist movement had lost its Polish flavor. In Czechoslovakia, on the other hand, the communists enjoyed at least as much popular support as the members of the government-in-exile who returned after the war. The Czechoslovak Communist party had been active before the war and had opposed Nazis and collaborators during the war. It preached national unity and exploited opposition to political leaders who had spent the war years abroad and who, rightly or wrongly, were identified both with the surrender at Munich and indifference toward the needs of the working class. Thus, the coalition governments established after the war became ever more vulnerable to communist pressure and could not ultimately resist the outright communist takeover ordered by Stalin in 1948. Finally, in Bulgaria and Albania democracy was never an issue after World War II. The majority of the Bulgarian people had been traditionally pro-Russian and knew little about their Soviet "liberators." In Albania, democracy was an unknown phenomenon since the 1930s, first under King Zog and later under Italian occupation. Enver Hoxha, the dogmatic Stalinist who assumed power in 1944, had opposition only from a few intellectuals whose relations with the Albanian masses were frail at best.

It is a matter of pure speculation under what conditions the countries of Eastern Europe would have been able to evolve democratic political and social orders after World War II. Had the Marshall Plan been extended to all of Europe, which might have occurred had Stalin adopted a different course, there might have been a possibility of gradual transition from authoritarianism and/or totalitarianism to democracy. It is possible to ascertain, however, the reasons for opposition to communist totalitarianism during the forty years of its existence and the impact of that totalitarianism on the political and socioeconomic culture of Eastern Europe.

The prevailing opposition to totalitarian communism of the Stalinist or neo-Stalinist varieties was motivated primarily by the elimination and/or limitation of private property rights and the corresponding pauperization of the populations at large. These factors, at least among the peasant and working classes, were more important than the severe restriction of personal liberty and abuse of human rights that characterized the communist regimes. Whereas the imposition of ideological conformity and consequent abrogation of freedom of expression were major determinants of the urban intellectuals' opposition to communism, the attack on religion, particularly in Orthodox and Catholic regions, precluded the ideological legitimation of communism with the rural masses.

From as early as 1951, Stalin and ethnic communist leaders sought to nationalize the communist regimes of Eastern Europe in an effort to seek identification of communism with the historic traditions of their respective states. Yet "socialist patriotism" never equaled historic nationalism. The communist leaders' attempts to claim legitimacy as executors of the national historic legacies and socioeconomic desiderata of the peoples were never persuasive to the vast majority of their citizens. Even in such extreme interpretations as those propounded by Nicolae Ceausescu in

Romania - who adopted the same heroes and identified the same enemies of the Romanians as did his fascist predecessors - communist nationalism was not regarded as representative of the national political culture. On the other hand, the leaders' identification with historic traditions kept alive, perhaps even regenerated, intra- and international confrontations and ethnic and religious conflicts suppressed in the early years of communist rule.

Such phenomena were most evident in Romania where systematic anti-Russian and anti-Hungarian propaganda on matters related to territorial rights in Bessarabia and Transylvania, respectively, and overt discrimination against ethnic minorities assumed major proportions in the later years of the Ceausescu regime. They were also evident in Bulgaria, where the Macedonian question and the persecution of the Turkish minority inflamed the spirits of nationalists, as well as in Yugoslavia where ethnic or religious questions focusing on Serbo-Albanian and Serbo-Croat relations assumed crisis proportions after Tito's death. Anti-Romanian propaganda in Hungary and uneasy relations between Czechs and Slovaks in Czechoslovakia surfaced periodically as well. In all Eastern European countries where nationalism was linked to Jewish questions, anti-Semitism was tolerated, if not encouraged, by communist rulers.

Other deleterious aspects of communist governance appear to have affected the reaction of the masses to their governments to a lesser degree. The destruction of the old ruling elites and bourgeoisie were generally taken in stride by the overwhelmingly agrarian and proletarian societies. The expansion of the bureaucracy, the creation of new privileged groups, the corruption of functionaries, excessive nepotism - all familiar phenomena of authoritarian rule - became intolerable only because the communists generally failed to undertake reforms that would have resulted in "socialism with a human face." Indeed, where such reforms were implemented, in Kádár's Hungary and Tito's Yugoslavia, "reformist" communism was found acceptable, at least for a while.

In view of these considerations, it is necessary to address the question raised at the beginning of this essay: Is Eastern Europe ready, willing, or able to be made safe for democracy as totalitarianism of the left has collapsed or is disintegrating?

The free use, or rather misuse, of the term *democracy* by parties involved in shaping the course of Eastern Europe in the post-totalitarian period renders a simple answer impossible. The contention that the various revolutions that removed neo-Stalinist, oppressive, and even moderate communist regimes were an expression of the people's quest for democracy is basically fallacious. Anti-communism was clearly the motivating force in the people's actions, but anti-communism does not necessarily represent a commitment to Western-style democracy.

After nearly a half-century of communist rule, political pluralism has no solid bases in the countries in question. The elites that evolved under communism, chiefly the bureaucratic state machine, the *apparat* and the *nomenklatura*, resemble the pre-communist bureaucracy in subservience to authority and lack of sympathy for Western democratic procedures and ideas. Nor are the armed forces, so important in the events of 1989, committed to democracy. The intellectuals who, together with students, played a leading role in overthrowing communist rule are not necessarily tolerant of diversity, and seem to support nationalism. Except in Czechoslovakia, urban intellectuals who were leaders or active participants in the movements that undermined and eventually removed the communists from power do not appear to enjoy the confidence of the masses. The link between the intellectuals and the masses tends to be anti-communist nationalism that, in many an instance, is assuming a xenophobic and/or anti-Semitic character. If the elections held in Eastern Europe in 1990 serve as a guide, it would appear that the working class and the peasantry are not enthusiastic about Western-style democratization. Their reasons are pragmatic and directly related to economic factors. Oppressive as communism may have been, it at least provided, albeit in a miserly manner, economic security. The introduction of a market economy, it is feared, would lead to massive unemployment and higher prices. Political pluralism is no substitute for perceived economic catastrophe for the traditionally apolitical and uneducated masses, never mind the assurances of eventual prosperity given by economists, political leaders, and entrepreneurs favoring free economies.

All these caveats are largely dismissed as irrelevant by interpreters of the historic evolution of Eastern Europe in the twentieth century who believe that communist totalitarianism had such a negative impact on Eastern Europe that its peoples would be willing to face new hardships and uncertainties inherent in political and economic restructuring to secure a democratic order. Realistically, however, the historic legacy of the twentieth century in general, and of the communist period in particular, mitigate against such optimism.

Taking stock of Eastern Europe in 1991, we find economically bankrupt states burdened by enormous foreign debts, inefficient and outdated industrial and agricultural systems, grave environmental problems, and a restless working class. Moreover, political instability related to problems of transition from entrenched communist totalitarianism to a pluralistic system appears to be more complex than assumed in the euphoria created by the events of 1989. The lack of experience of the newly formed or reactivated pre-totalitarian political organizations is probably less significant in this respect than matters related to their ability to secure the confidence of the population. The brutalizing of the peoples of Eastern Europe by communist totalitarianism has frightened the electorate and brought out its immediate self-interest. Under the circumstances, people voted on the basis of personal fears and prejudices for those whom they believed most likely to be able to remedy existing evils. For democracy to succeed it would have to remove fears and alleviate prejudices. In other words, it would have to alter the political and socio-economic order and culture. That would be a monumental task given the circumstances in contemporary Eastern Europe.

Present conditions are no better for making Eastern Europe safe for democracy than they were at the end of World War I. If economic prosperity, presumably assured by a market economy, is essential for democracy, the prospects are grim. The highly competitive capitalist economies of Western Europe, the United States, and Japan are only marginally interested in providing economic assistance or in developing markets in heavily indebted countries with worthless currencies, inefficient work forces, and obsolete industrial plants. And even if, for reasons unrelated to the furthering of democracy, they would decide to penetrate the markets of Eastern Europe, it would take a long time before the economies of those countries would be able to ensure the well-being ostensibly guaranteed by market economies. It seems fair to say that economic solutions provided by means other than free economic systems are likely to be adopted, or continued, in most of Eastern Europe.

It could be argued, of course, that a socialist economy is not necessarily an impediment to the attainment of political democracy. In fact, socialism and democracy are compatible. Functional socialist economies may be to the liking of East Europeans. Still, transition from communist-style planning and economic development to socialism would require a greater financial input by the major capitalist countries of the world than those countries probably can or will assure.

Even if we were to assume that the prospect of slow advancement toward free market or socialist economies would be a price the peoples of Eastern Europe would be willing to pay for democracy, we should ask ourselves whether the accompanying changes in these peoples' political and social cultures are likely to occur in the foreseeable future.

The answer is: probably not. The anti-communism of the East Europeans has, if anything, strengthened the traditional role played by religion and religious institutions in their lives. Since the view that heathen communism in association with anti-Christian Judaism were responsible for the evils that befell Eastern Europe after World War I has resurfaced and is being promoted by anti-communist and nationalist politicians, intellectuals, and often émigrés, anti-Semitism is on the rise. This, in conjunction with the nationalism engendered by the communists and later by the labeling of the movements that led to the collapse of the communist regimes as "national revolutions," has not advanced the spirit of toleration of ethnic or religious diversity so essential for the promotion of democracy.

Finally, in a period of economic uncertainty, of getting even with previous oppressors, of social readjustment, and of general nervousness and insecurity, national and international reconciliation and political stability in general are not likely to be recorded soon. It is doubtful that totalitarianism of the communist variety would recur, but authoritarianism, paternalist or even militaristic, cannot be excluded as an alternative to (potential) democracy should economic conditions deteriorate. Only if the economies of Eastern Europe gradually improve and eventually even prosper could democracy - socialist or laissez-faire capitalist - take root before the end of the century. In the meantime, it is not enough to use the slogan "We shall overcome;" rather we should address the ever-pertinent question "What's to be done?"

CHAPTER TWO

EAST CENTRAL EUROPE:
CONTINUITY AND CHANGE

In their constant effort to justify their deviation from Russian interpretations of Marxism-Leninism, the contemporary rulers of the countries of East Central Europe have rewritten the "laws of history." They invoke the national historical traditions, minimizing and rationalizing the incompatibilities between these and communist internationalism. They propound the theory that the routes to communism are multiple and should be determined by the "specific historical conditions" of individual countries, whether inherited by the communists from the *anciens régimes* or created by the new socialist order. Even when they cite national historical legacies as a mandate for communism, they are, in effect, justifying continuation of state nationalism and opposition to political and economic vassalage disguised as supranational communism. In one form or another, the rulers of all countries of East Central Europe, with the possible exception of Bulgaria, are nationalists in communists' clothing.

The rewriting of national histories to conform to contemporary political requirements is man-made, from above; the new versions do not reflect the real nature of the process of historical continuity and change, do not differentiate between myth and reality. This is not to say that there has been no historical continuity in the twentieth century or that the communist regimes of Eastern Europe are merely externally-imposed, unrooted, dictatorships manned by interchangeable functionaries of international communism. But the historical record does not, contrary to the assertion of the present rulers of Eastern Europe, show that the elements of continuity and identification have been the communist parties, which the leaders claim are fulfillers of the social and (whenever convenient) national revolutionary actions and aspirations of the masses. In fact, even the common denominator of continuity, nationalism, has been transformed in a "communist solution" into a blend essentially different from that of prewar years.

It is a mistake to regard "bourgeois nationalism" as a forerunner of "communist nationalism," even if certain elements of the former have been incorporated into the latter. Historical East European nationalism and communism of any variety are not miscible. When combined in their pure form - as in Hungary in 1956 - they lead to explosion; even when diluted, they remain in a curious state of suspension with the heavier component, communism, always on top. The exploitation of bourgeois nationalism by the communist rulers has necessarily been selective. In Rumania, for instance, it has been limited to rekindling traditional anti-Russian and anti-Hungarian sentiments as convenient for the pursuit of the regime's "independent course." In Hungary, on the other hand, the experience of 1956 permitted only the reviving of anti-Rumanian irredentism. Gomulka's adaptation encourages only traditional anti-Germanism, ignoring the fact that Russia's historic role has not been that of a friend of the Polish people. The Bulgarian communists have had no such problems as their country's nationalist tradition supports friendship with the Russians. The fulminations of the Albanians against the "revisionists" in the Kremlin are, whatever the dialectics, identical with the anti-Greek and anti-Yugoslav manifestations of prewar years.

Other integral ingredients of prewar nationalism have been tolerated only in cases of extreme necessity. Its very essence, anti-communism, has been under constant attack. Its ideological foundations have been undermined, its religious rationale condemned. But no matter how ruthless the initial persecution of its exponents - fascists, democrats, liberals, socialists, peasants, intellectuals, clergymen, landowners, bureaucrats, businessmen, merchants, technocrats - the communists had to make their peace with their people. The process of buying off the masses by channeling traditional prejudices, current discontent and unfulfilled aspirations into the mainstream of "socialist patriotism" and "economic nationalism" has been far-reaching. But it has not rooted out the bases of historical East European nationalism.

Certainly, Gomulkaism and Titoism are uneasy and incomplete syntheses. The concessions made in Poland to the most powerful anti-communist forces, the Catholic Church and the peasantry, have not resulted in acceptance of the new national *raison d'être*, anti-German propaganda notwithstanding. And even if the intense conflict between Serb and Croat, Catholic and Orthodox, town and village has progressed from blood feud to economic and bureaucratic backstabbing, unity in the name of independence from foreign domination and the creation of a united communist national state have hardly been achieved. Elsewhere in Eastern Europe, where forcible agricultural collectivization has been carried out, as it has not in Poland and Yugoslavia, communist nationalism rests on even more precarious foundations. It has only the most limited acceptance among the peasant masses which, despite their disappointment in the peasant and fascist movements of the interwar years, remain opposed to communism, nationalist or not. It is resented by national minorities and Jews fearful of discrimination. The "socialist patriotism" of the intellectuals and professional cadres is skin-deep, acceptable only as an evil lesser than communist internationalism. For ultimately, whether converted socialists, democrats, fascists, or disillusioned communists, the educated are aware of the incompatibility between traditional nationalism and communism, between the still supreme national interest - freedom from communism - and the true *raison d'être* of communist nationalism - survival of the communist power elite.

But communist nationalism - child of a Stalinist father and a "fascist" mother - provides a framework for a viable society, for peaceful coexistence between rulers and subjects. The rulers have chosen the easiest and most understandable course to secure at last a *modus vivendi* with their own people: fulfillment of their economic desiderata through the building of the "nationalist socialist" society. However, the principal manifestation of the new nationalism, the quest for economic independence, is the weakest element of the national historical traditions. Even if protectionism was a basic feature of prewar East European economics, the root cause of international conflict was territorial irredentism or revisionism, not economic competition. Economic collaboration was invariably a function of political relations. It is, of course, possible that the industrialization of East European societies would have led to more significant economic rivalries and the emergence of economic nationalism along contemporary lines even with the subjugation of Eastern Europe by Communist Russia. In fact, however, economic nationalism has been created by the communist rulers of East Central Europe often without an economic rationale. Tito's economic nationalism was forced upon him by political differences with Moscow. So was Hoxha's and, to a lesser degree, Gheorghiu-Dej's. Kadar's economic nationalism, much less pronounced, was derived from the political events of 1956. So, in a way, was Gomulka's. Only Novotny's is based on valid economic considerations. But it must not be forgotten that the Czechs were the strongest supporters of economic internationalism, through COMECON, even if this position reflected the arrogance and exigencies of a developed economy. Economic nationalism is thus generally political in origin and, as such, earns what popular support it has.

In recognizing the unifying force of nationalism, the rulers of Eastern Europe have had to make further compromises with the historical legacy. If the national goal is the creation of the economically powerful, independent communist state, reliance on the nation's resources has become necessarily greater than in the days of Stalinist dogmatism and unadulterated Russian imperialism. In the process of accelerated national socialist construction, so evident in the last few years, the removal of the professional barriers previously imposed on technocrats, bureaucrats and intellectuals of bourgeois or even aristocratic origin has been recognized as essential to progress. With the exception of Albania, the class struggle has *de facto* ended and the *ci-devants* reintegrated into the new technological-bureaucratic society. In some countries - Poland, Czechoslovakia, Hungary, and even Rumania - the "new society," granted the basic changes resultant from industrialization, looks and acts remarkably like the old. Social mobility from below has been gradually slowed down with the result that the professional cadres entrusted with the direction and execution of "socialist construction" consist primarily of individuals who had either continued in their prewar positions or were reinstated following disgrace and professional ostracism and, perhaps more significantly, of sons and daughters of the "class enemy." This phoenix phenomenon is most evident in the composition of the intelligentsia: the "old guard" is solidly entrenched and nepotism is the rule. There is hardly an academician in Eastern Europe today who could or would boast of pure peasant or proletarian descent.

"Unhealthy" social origin has been given a clean bill of health; even more, it has actually become respectable and useful. The *embourgeoise-ment* of the industrial elite and of the urban bureaucracy of proletarian background is not new. The worker-politician has imitated the bourgeois way of life for nearly twenty years but discarded the cap for the felt hat only after his country committed itself to national communism and began to seek recognition and economic assistance from the West. In the past five years, and longer in Yugoslavia and Poland, prewar social patterns and behavior have become more and more evident in the capital cities and white collar community in general. But the *communiste gentilhomme* remains basically communist. The true power elite, the proletarian core of the parties' central committees, politbureaus, and secretariats, is concerned by the contradiction between communist theory and political reality. It is aware that the East European worker and peasant are still generally unable to provide the leading cadres necessary for successful socialist construction, that the national goal cannot be achieved solely through the efforts of illiterates or semi-literates. It is disturbed by the reclassification of society along modified prewar lines. It is uneasy over its own dependence on political agnostics for execution of long-range plans. Men like Ceausescu,

Zhivkov, Gomulka, Kadar or Novotny are certainly more comfortable in negotiating directly with their counterparts in the "socialist camp" than through presentable "front men" with the West. With obvious discomfiture, they tolerate the reappearance of Western cultural influences. But ultimately they realize that exclusive reliance on the Soviet Union and doctrinaire communism is more inimical to their own interests than compromise with the internal "class enemy" and the "forces of imperialism," at least as long as they can effectively control the course of events in their countries.

The interaction between the engineers and the architects of socialist construction has so far resulted only in minimal compromises. The power elite has made no fundamental concessions on major issues of policy, and has not permitted the alteration of its structure to include elements that would shift the balance of power in favor of the non-proletarian. As a rule, the technocrat and the intellectual remain subordinated to the worker-politician at the decision-making level. They are also a minority in the party organization *per se* where the industrial worker and peasant enjoy an overwhelming majority. The technocrats' and intellectuals' cooperation is essential for the development of the nationalist communist state, and their influence is out of proportion to their numerical strength in the party. They are, however, unlikely to penetrate the inner sanctum of power or to erode the rigidity characteristic of all the East European systems.

The technocrats are advisers rather than policy makers, executors of political decisions even where such decisions are contrary to economic or technological rationale. They are innovators only to the extent permitted by the Central Committee. They are the "kept women" of a technologically-oriented power elite with *entrée* at the pleasure of the politbureaus and secretariats. They are divorced from the masses frequently by social origin, always by privileged status, but accepted by them as an essential link in the construction of a more acceptable society. The role of the intellectuals is more limited though similar. They provide ideological justification for pragmatic political action. They translate the dicta of the political oligarchies into all languages and forms of intellectual expression. They are instruments for conferring international prestige on the ruling elites and serve as liaison men to the population at large. Although their freedom of expression has increased markedly in Poland, Yugoslavia, Hungary, Rumania and Czechoslovakia, it is still limited by the prescription, "nationalist" in form and "socialist" in content; thus the tie with national cultural traditions is at best formal. The overstepping of ideological boundaries is not tolerated, except occasionally in Yugoslavia and, with increasing rarity, in Poland. The influence and subservience of intellectuals assure them of the privileged status they now enjoy but not of the respect of the masses. To the latter they are less essential than the technocrats, certainly less likely to alter the course of socialist construction.

Useful as the practicing technocrat and intellectual may be to the parties, they are nevertheless bypassed in the process of power elite formation. Dependence on the former could at a certain level of industrial development result in the transformation of doctrinaire communist planning into scientific socialist planning, an undesirable alternative for the present rulers. Anti-intellectualism limits the intellectual's mobility in the party ranks. Only the tested, long-standing member of the party organizations belonging to the technocracy or intelligentsia may hope to reach the higher echelons of the communist order, since the ruling elite replenishes its ranks from the party bureaucracy. Whether this bureaucracy be largely of peasant origin as in Bulgaria, or proletarian as in Czechoslovakia or Rumania, or mixed and interspersed with bourgeois intellectuals and technocrats, the essential fact is that the process of coterie formation is rigidly limited and controlled by the worker-politician currently in command of the party and state apparatus in all countries except underdeveloped Albania. The rigorously screened bureaucratic cadres insure the continuity of the power elite and its political decisions and thus the ultimate control of all aspects of socialist construction. The bureaucracy is not identified with or representative of the interests of any social class or professional group other than the party *apparatchik*. It is the rigid guardian of the party's vested interests, the conservative opponent of innovation, ideological and institutional. It is symbolic of communist rather than historical continuity, of historical rather than communist change.

An appraisal of contemporary East Central Europe shows profound changes from and only basic continuity with the interwar years. The communist regimes are fundamentally different from their predecessors. The East European revolution was completed by the mid-fifties and whatever changes have occurred since that time are post-revolutionary. Contemporary Eastern Europe bears a closer resemblance to that of the thirties than it did ten years ago, but such resemblance is a superficial one. The process of change is directed by communist parties, which have not changed substantially since early Stalinist days, and results from commitment to industrialization and problems related to the "socialist transformation" of their countries. As a rule the personnel of the power elite today is either the same as in the late forties and early fifties or recruited from cadres active in that period. In each party organization the power rests with men who could, in case of necessity, readily revert to practices they have publicly condemned since 1956. The party and governmental machinery and institutions have remained virtually unchanged since Stalin's days and few meaningful innovations in "socialist construction" have taken place. "Liberalization" and "humanization," terms used to characterize the nature of political change in East Central Europe, are used in juxtaposition to Stalinism rather than to prewar conditions.

Change can be observed in the quest for economic and political independence from Russia, but this process of partial disengagement takes place *en famille*, among members of the "socialist camp." It is in no way comparable to the anti-Bolshevik, anti-Soviet tradition of pre-communist Eastern Europe. The very notion of a "rapprochement" with the West reveals the distance Eastern Europe has traveled from its traditional political orientation and alignments; it is perhaps as striking as its involvement in the Sino-Soviet conflict and Southeast Asian affairs and the political consequences of non-European factors on the countries of the area.

As the process of change becomes more pronounced in East Central Europe under the impact of industrialization, as the disintegration of the village and the increase in the proletariat proceeds, the differences between interwar and communist Eastern Europe will be further accentuated. The links with the "bourgeois-capitalist" and agrarian past, currently maintained by the peasantry and intelligentsia more than by the technocracy and industrial working class, are likely to be restricted to identification with a national heritage, cultural and historical. In the current period of transition from unicentric international Stalinism to polycentric international communism, in the process of growth of the national communist state and of the "socialist community" on the basis of association of individual members, the element of historical continuity is emphasized and apparent. But it must not be forgotten that the historical legacy of the twenties and thirties is respected and valid only insofar as it contributes to the execution of plans and to the creation of societies based on blueprints alien to the historical tradition.

CHAPTER THREE

THE BOLSHEVIK REVOLUTION
AND BALKAN REVOLUTIONS

If we were to believe contemporary interpretations of the role played by the Bolshevik Revolution first in influencing, and then in shaping, the course of Balkan revolutionary activities since World War I, we would have to conclude that the triumph of communism in the Balkans in our times was entirely a function of the fulfillment of the revolutionary aspirations of the peoples of the Balkans, under the guidance and inspiration provided by the Russian prototype. Such a contention is essentially baseless. Nevertheless, given the outcome of the Balkan peoples' "struggle for independence," the relationship between the Soviet Union and the Balkan countries assumes paramount importance in any assessment of the relationship between the Bolshevik Revolution and Balkan revolutions.

Until 1917 Balkan revolutionary activities could be characterized primarily as movements designed to secure, first, national independence, and second, the loosely defined historic goals of the Balkan nations. Most of these goals were defined by the leadership as realization of the historic aspirations of the Balkan peoples, focusing on the peoples' right to enjoy once more the benefits of independence and well-being which their historic ancestors had enjoyed in preconquest times. The connotations were essentially nationalist, generally ignoring the social and economic desiderata of the masses. The subordination of the attainment of socioeconomic goals to the realization of national independence was willy-nilly tolerated by the Balkan peoples and, in such cases where the interests of the masses differed from those of the leadership, the leadership was either able to suppress the aspirations of the masses or the masses failed to lend full support to the revolutionary movements, with resultant failure of the leaders' goals. There were very few social revolutionary actions, at odds with the liberation struggles proclaimed by the leadership, recorded in the nineteenth and early twentieth centuries. In fact, probably the only such manifestation which attained more than ordinary status in the record of Balkan revolutionary activity, was the Great Peasant Revolt of 1907 in the Romanian Kingdom.[1]

To qualify the Revolt of 1907 as a social revolution is probably in error, in that it was a spontaneous jacquerie, albeit of major proportions. It was the ultimate expression of frustration by the Romanian peasantry, which of all peasantries in the Balkans received least satisfaction from the ruling class, despite formal emancipation in 1864 and massive peasant participation in the Romanian War of Independence in 1877-78. The suppression of the uprising by the Romanian army was more important than the vague promises of reform and eventual fulfillment of the basic demands of the rebels upon attainment of the ultimate national goal - the establishment of Greater Romania. This brief discourse on the Revolt of 1907 is essential in any attempt to link social revolutionary manifestations in the Balkans with the Bolshevik Revolution of 1917, since there was indeed an intimate relationship between the Bolshevik Revolution as manifested in Bessarabia in 1917 and the de facto revolution which occurred among the Romanian peasantry, drafted into the Romanian army, shortly after the outbreak of the October Revolution in Russia. The Bessarabian example served to provoke demands for genuine emancipation and distribution of Romanian land to the peasantry, voiced by the rank and file of the Romanian peasant army, and, in turn, led to acceptance of these demands by King Ferdinand and the ensuing social transformation of Romania at the end of World War I. But did this sequence of actions and events indeed represent a meaningful link between the Bolshevik Revolution and the Balkan revolutionary tradition? Our answer would have to be negative on at least two counts. The Romanian peasants had no perception of the character of the Bolshevik Revolution or of its aims. They responded in the same manner as the Russian peasants did when promised land and peace by the cynical leaders of the Bolshevik Revolution. Moreover, the Romanian peasantry had no love for left-wing political movements since, despite the perception of the significance of the Revolt of 1907 by the leading Romanian socialist of the time, Constantin Dobrogeanu-Gherea, the socialists had no commitment to peasant uprisings or, for that matter, to satisfying the "petit-bourgeois" desires of the Romanian peasantry.[2]

The same question could also be asked with respect to the similar revolutionary manifestations which occurred in Bulgaria in 1918, again allegedly under the impact of the October Revolution. It is true that the Bulgarian actions were far more political than the Romanian in that the Left-Wing Socialists and the Agrarians who were behind the revolutionary movement had greater political experience than the Social Democrats of Romania. It is noteworthy, however, that the Bulgarian peasant units in the army were far more responsive to the entreaties of the Agrarian Union than to those of the Left-Wing Socialists, and that ultimately the temporarily successful uprising of September 1918, headed by Raiko Dascalov, resulted in the assumption of power, again albeit temporarily, by the head of the Agrarian Union, Aleksandr Stamboliski.[3] It is also noteworthy that after the defeat of the revolutionaries by the loyal army, supported by German forces, in October, it was the Agrarians, and not the Left-Wing Socialists (who had formed the Bulgarian Communist Party in 1919), who secured the support of the peasantry for the peaceful political revolution which brought Stamboliski to power as head of a legally elected government in October 1919. By that time, the Communists were suspect and uncooperative and the Bulgarian masses sought solutions to political and economic problems totally opposed to those advocated by the Bulgarian Communists and practiced by Moscow.

In fact, Stamboliski's governance was characterized by peasant rule for the peasantry in a manner radically opposed to the political aims of both the right and the left. Peasant democracy was intolerable to the Bulgarian Communist Party and to its mentors in the Kremlin, as it negated the assumptions and corollary policies adopted in the Soviet Union in a manner so detrimental to the aspirations of the peasant masses. Thus, when the Bulgarian right staged the coup of June 9, 1923, which overthrew the Agrarian government, put down ruthlessly the pro-Stamboliski peasant uprisings in various parts of Bulgaria, and in the process murdered Stamboliski himself, the Bulgarian Communist Party remained neutral. The neutrality was an expression of the anti-peasant policies of the Communists as much as of the Party's realization that the peasants had no interest in a Communist solution to their problems. The belated attempt to refuel the revolutionary spirit of the pro-Stamboliski masses in September 1923 through the staging of a Communist, worker-led, revolution of the restless peasantry failed miserably. The defeat of the September Uprising by the military forces of the Tsankov government was indeed facilitated by the lack of peasant support for the Communist-directed revolution as well as by greater identification of the peasants' interests with the "reactionary" Tsankov regime than with the "revolutionary" Bulgarian Communist leadership.

The only strata of Bulgarian, and for that matter also of Romanian, society which were in any way responsive to the ideology and practices of the Bolshevik Revolution were small segments of the industrial proletariat and of the intellectuals but, by and large, even within these groups there were defections to the right, or even outright identification with the radical revolutionary right, which strongly overshadowed a class commitment to left-wing revolutionary plans or programs. And there were good reasons for this.

The original illusions entertained by ignorant and restless peasants and "democratically" oriented intellectuals regarding the goals expounded by the Bolsheviks in Russia and by President Woodrow Wilson in his master plan for the pacification of the world, were shattered by the realities of the Bolshevik order in Russia and the rejection of Wilsonianism by political leaders in the United States and Western Europe. As the forces of nationalism reemerged - with a corresponding revival of territorial revisionism and small power imperialism - justification for rejection of democratic reforms with corresponding alterations in the socioeconomic structures of the Balkan countries was provided by revisionism and counter-revisionism, as well as by the threat of communism; the defense and propagation of national interest threatened by Russian communism and traditional foreign enemies became the raison d'être of the rulers of the Balkans. The overthrow of Stamboliski's regime was the watershed in Bulgaria and, for that matter, it was symbolic of Balkan developments in general. Tsankov's regime, supported by and supportive of the IMRO, provided the rationale for the pursuit of "revolutionary activities" by that revolutionary organization committed to the "liberation" of Macedonia and other disputed Bulgarian territories from "national enemies." And indeed, most of the conservative classes in Bulgaria, while not entirely supportive of IMRO extremism, did endorse the goal of defending and furthering Bulgarian national interests as most suitable to the attainment of their own social, economic, and political interests.[4] And this was also true in Romania, where the emancipation of the peasantry, the granting of political rights to Jews, and the threat of Soviet, Hungarian, and Bulgarian revisionisms were parlayed into political actions and organizations designed to maintain the interests of the conservative forces to the detriment of the peasants, Jews, and national minorities. In Romania, however, the left was weak and vulnerable on account of the heavily Jewish preponderance in the Communist and Social Democratic parties. The cause of the peasant, theoretically expounded by the various peasant parties, was advanced very precariously because of the intrinsic opposition to peasant interests by the conservative ruling groups. Therefore, a populist, revolutionary right emerged slowly in the early twenties as the forerunner of the radical, revolutionary, populist movement later identified with the Iron Guard. The forerunners of the Iron Guard, headed by the same Corneliu Zelea Codreanu and his young associates, advocated a radical anti-Semitic, anti-

Communist program, ostensibly favoring the improvement of the economic and social conditions of the peasantry and the rallying of the masses for a national Christian crusade for the preservation of the integrity of Greater Romania threatened by a Judeo-Communist conspiracy, by pro-Jewish political leaders, and by foreign revisionists. And this extreme right-wing populist movement enjoyed, from its very inception in the twenties, a significant amount of support from disgruntled intellectuals, students, bureaucrats, and even the younger members of the peasantry. Thus, the IMRO and the Legion of Archangel Michael were, in their own ways, revolutionary organizations with a certain *prise* in their respective countries. And their bases of support were stronger than those of the revolutionary left.[5]

Rightist revolutionary actions and programs were not unique to Bulgaria and Romania. They were evident in Greece when, at the height of the frustration over the defeat suffered at the hands of the Turks, the Revolutionary Committee headed by Colonel Nicholas Plastiras seized power late in 1922 ostensibly to defend the national interests and ambitions of the Greeks.[6] And again in 1926 and 1935, military revolts directed against constitutionalism, against communism, and against revisionism were recorded. It is true that the military movements were not necessarily representative of the interests of the majority of the Greek population, but they were not repudiated by that population either, as they were carried out in the name of supporting and reinforcing the ever-present Greek nationalism and its revendications.

Albania, too, was not free of nationalist-determined revolutionary activities after World War I.[7] The revolt organized by the Committee of National Defense in the district of Vlora in 1920 against Italian occupiers of several Albanian districts may not have been either rightist or leftist, considering the low level of political consciousness of the Albanians. But it was clearly an expression of Albanian nationalism. And even the far more political revolution of June 1924, directed against Ahmet Zog and his ruling "Zogist clique" by a motley coalition headed by Fan Noli, with the cooperation of regional military commanders and with the support of the illiterate Albanian masses, was not devoid of nationalist overtones. Zog was indeed characterized by Fan Noli and his left-wing supporters as an oppressor of the rights and liberties of the Albanian people, and, in truth, Noli looked upon the uprising as a social revolution against rule by a dominant clique of landlords and conservative military forces. The other participants, however, were persuaded to join the movement on the basis of

Zog's being a traitor to the interests of the Albanian people because of his ties with Yugoslavia, Greece, and Italy - all mortal foreign enemies of Albania. The actual defeat of the revolution by forces loyal to Zog was facilitated by the strains and stresses within the revolutionary camp when Noli's leftist tendencies clashed with the simpler social and economic demands of the peasantry and the distinctly anti-Soviet positions adopted by the conservative allies in the revolutionary coalition. In a sense, then, Noli's revolutionary program, moderate though it may have been, was as unacceptable to the majority of his followers as was his gradual abandonment of nationalist positions in favor of a distinctly pro-Soviet orientation.

It would be fallacious to argue that social unrest was not prevalent among various social groups, some of which favored communist-style solutions. There were strikes and other violent manifestations by workers, most notably in Romania. The so-called Grivița Uprising by Romania's railway workers in 1933 was indicative of the social and economic crisis of the working class, but it did not per se represent unequivocal acceptance of Soviet solutions. Rather, in Romania and, for that matter, also in Yugoslavia in the thirties, resolution of social and political conflicts were more readily sought within the framework of right-wing formulas. The Romanian Iron Guard flourished in the thirties and enjoyed much support from the working class and working peasantry. Similarly, Croat separatists enjoyed wide support from the population of Croatia in their attempts to assert the values of Croatian nationalism and to protect the interests of the Croatian population in the face of Serbian domination. And even in Greece, where the Communist party had significant following among many an intellectual and the disgruntled proletariat, and in Bulgaria, where Dimitrov's heroics and adverse economic conditions evoked favorable responses from certain segments of the working class, Communist solutions - even when couched in nationalist formulas - were rejected by the overwhelming majority of the population. The changing tactics of the left-wing revolutionaries in favor of united fronts and democratic action programs in defense of the national interests of the peoples of the Balkans were ineffectual until, indeed, the territorial integrity and national interests of the majority of the Balkan nations were placed in mortal jeopardy by the actions of the Axis powers. And those actions ultimately accounted for the success of revolutionary movements led by Communists in Greece, Albania, and Yugoslavia, and for the imposing of Communist revolutionary solutions to the problems of Romania and Bulgaria during World War II.

The crux of the matter in appraising the ties between Communist revolution and the Balkan revolutionary tradition lies in the appraisal of the nature of the anti-Fascist "wars of liberation" which occurred during the Second World War, and which paved the way to the establishment of Communist regimes in all of the Balkan countries except Greece. The claims and counter-claims are well-known but are worth summarizing. Official doctrine, as expounded by Balkan historians today, is simply that the armed opposition movements to German, Italian, and native "fascist" forces were in fact spontaneous social-revolutionary manifestations, triggered by dissatisfied masses and by Communists, the latter as rightful representatives of the masses' interests. The wars of liberation were also national movements, reflecting the peoples' determination to rid their countries of fascist oppressors and their desire to assure the territorial integrity and national independence of sought-after Communist national states.

These claims are specious, as there is no evidence to substantiate the validity of the ultimate equation of national independence and Communist rule. It is true, at least in the case of Yugoslavia and Greece, and to a lesser extent also Albania, that the resistance movements to German and/or Italian occupation were spontaneous mass movements by patriotic and abused peasants, workers, intellectuals, and other social groups.[8] It is also true that the Communists soon assumed a primary role in leading the resistance movements and were successful in that role to the extent to which they expounded programs and goals originally compatible with the interests of the masses. The accent, in the decisive phases of the wars of liberation, was indeed on patriotic motivation and on eventual social reform rather than on Communist revolution. Only as leaders of patriotic movements could the Communist leaders of Tito's partisans, or of ELAS in Greece, hope to retain the support of their non-Communist followers. In fact, however, the essential goal of the Communists, from as soon as the defeat of the Axis could be anticipated, was to destroy all political forces which could oppose the transformation of the war of liberation into a war for the establishment of Communist rule in Yugoslavia, Greece, and Albania. Thus, the primary targets of the Communist leaders became the *Cetniks* in Yugoslavia, EDDES and EKKA in Greece, and all potential internal opponents of the *Balli Kombëtar* in Albania - all grouped together with other "domestic reactionaries," such as the *Ustasha*, traditional political parties, or other ostensible supporters of the Italian or German forces still active in the Peninsula. And not far behind in the list of priorities was the consolidation of the bases of future political power of Communist leaders at the expense of the majority of their followers, whose postwar aspirations were, for the Communists, incompatible with their own. It mattered little whether in this process Soviet tutelage and advice was to be sought, accepted, or received; what did matter was that the pattern of the wars of liberation in Yugoslavia, Albania, and Greece was tactically identical with that devised and used by the Bolsheviks first in 1917 and as needed thereafter.

The ultimate resolution of these overt and covert movements and conflicts was made not by the revolutionaries but by the Allies themselves. In Greece, where the Kremlin was unable to press its advantage in the face of British and American opposition, the communists were unable to "liberate" the country in the manner which they had contemplated. In Yugoslavia, the withdrawal of support from Mihailović's *Cetniks* by the British and Americans paved the way for Tito's ultimate success. And as Albania, Romania, and Bulgaria were considered by the Western Allies to be outside the sphere of their interests, these countries were "liberated" in a Communist manner. Liberation came to Albania mostly because of Yugoslav and Russian support of the "liberation" movement; and to Romania and Bulgaria, where resistance and "liberation" movements were indeed of minimal importance, by direct action by Stalin's armies and political representatives.[9] By 1945, imposed Communist revolutions became irreversible in the Balkans outside of Greece and, in theory, the bases for the ultimate achievement of the alleged eternal revolutionary goal of the peoples of the Balkans - national independence in a Communist state - had been laid in granite. And consolidation has continued ever since.

ENDNOTES

1. *Marea rascoala a taranilor din 1907* (Bucharest: 1967); Philip G. Eidelberg, *The Great Rumanian Peasant Revolt of 1907* (Leiden: Brill, 1974).
2. V. Liveanu, et al., *Relatii agrare si miscari taranesti în România 1908-1921* (Bucharest: 1967).
3. Joseph Rothschild, *The Communist Party of Bulgaria: Origins and Development, 1883-1936* (New York: Columbia University Press, 1959); Nissan Oren, *Bulgarian Communism: The Road to Power, 1934-1944* (New York: Columbia University Press, 1971); John D. Bell, *Peasants in Power: Alexander Stamboliski and the Bulgarian Agrarian Union, 1899-1923* (Princeton: Princeton University Press, 1977).
4. See especially Joseph Swire, *Bulgarian Conspiracy* (London: Ryerson, 1939).

5. Note 4 above and Henry L. Roberts, *Rumania: Political Problems of an Agrarian State* (New Haven: Yale University Press, 1951) and Eugen Weber, "Romania," in Hans Rogger and Eugen Weber, eds., *The European Right: A Historical Profile* (Berkeley: University of California Press, 1965), pp. 501-74.

6. Michael Llwellyn Smith, *Ionian Vision: Greece in Asia Minor, 1919-1922* (London: St. Martin's Press, 1973); D. George Kousoulas, *Revolution and Defeat: The Story of the Greek Communist Party* (London: Oxford University Press, 1965).

7. Kristo Frasheri, *The History of Albania* (Tirana: 1964), pp. 213ff.

8. John Hondros, *Occupation and Resistance: The Greek Agony, 1941-1944* (New York: 1979); Dominique Eudes, *The Kapetanios: Partisans and Civil War in Greece, 1943-1949* (London: Monthly Review, 1972); Peter R. Prifti, "The Labor Party of Albania," in Stephen Fischer-Galati, ed., *The Communist Parties of Eastern Europe* (New York: Columbia University Press, 1979), pp. 5ff; Frasheri, *History of Albania*, pp. 267ff; Jozo Tomasevich, *The Chetniks: War and Revolution in Yugoslavia, 1941-1945* (Stanford: Stanford University Press, 1975).

9. Thomas T. Hammond, ed., *The Anatomy of Communist Takeovers* (New Haven: Yale University Press, 1975), pp. 244-338.

CHAPTER FOUR

ROMANIA'S DEVELOPMENT
AS A COMMUNIST STATE

Perspectives for Romania's development in the 1980s are uncertain. They are less a function of factors related to the announced goals of the regime than of interpretations of successes or failures by Romanian and foreign political leaders, scholars, and propagandists. The ambiguity of this statement is reflective of the entire course of Romania's development as a communist state.

It is a continuing matter of dispute among actual or self-styled connoisseurs of Romanian affairs as to whether Romania has benefited from communist rule and planning, and whether or not a multilaterally-developed Romanian economy and society is emerging after nearly forty years since the liberation of the country by the Soviet Union in 1944. There is also doubt as to whether communist Romania has actually achieved meaningful independence in the pursuit of a foreign policy of its own, or whether the rule of Nicolae Ceausescu has been beneficial to Romanian modernization and to world peace. And, finally, there are questions regarding Romania's future in the 1980s even among supporters and defenders of Ceausescu's independent course who, like skeptics and detractors, foresee a rough road ahead in a decade of economic stagnation, political conflict, and aggravated energy crises.

It is difficult to find the *juste milieu* because of Romania's peculiar position in the communist and non-communist worlds. This is to say that the foreign policies pursued by Nicolae Ceausescu and by his immediate predecessor, Gheorghe Gheorghiu-Dej, have both conditioned and obscured internal realities so as to render objective assessment of the nature and development of communist Romania extremely difficult. Thus, any such assessment of the true character of Romania's development as a communist state and any prognoses for development in the 1980s revolve on an appraisal of Ceausescu's motives for the pursuit of policies of rapid multilateral development at home and of an independent foreign policy during the last fifteen years.

It has been said often that the ultimate purpose of Ceausescu's rule is the transformation of Romania, before the end of the twentieth century, into a multilaterally-developed, modern, independent, "national" communist state. There can be little doubt that rapid, altogether too rapid, industrialization has occurred in Romania since World War II. Statistical data are truly impressive per se and in terms of comparative achievement under pre-communist and communist rule. Yet, at the beginning of the 1980s the Romanian economy is in disarray, plagued by shortages of raw materials and hard currency, by enormous trade deficits, inadequate food supplies, and inflation. Although many of these symptoms can be attributed to global economic and political factors beyond Romania's control, not all of such ills can be explained by external conditions. The ultimate question is whether rapid, multilateral industrialization was actually necessary in Romania, or whether it is justifiable in any rational economic terms. Expert opinion is divided in these respects. However, communist modernization in Romania has never been a function of economic considerations alone. In fact, it seems fair to say that the socialist transformation of Romania from a retarded agricultural society into an advanced industrial one, thoroughly documented by Marvin Jackson in this volume, was at all times predicated on rather basic political considerations.

The industrialization of Romania antedates the communist era. It is true that until World War II, Romania's economy was primarily agricultural and that extractive industries were more developed than others. It is also true that the Romanians' standard of living was among the lowest in Europe. Be this as it may, plans for industrial development were drawn and even implemented in the twenties, thirties, and early forties by political forces other than the communists. Paul Shapiro discusses in the following chapter, for example, the interwar political development entirely outside a Marxist party. In fact, during those years, there was little communist commitment to anything but revolutionary activities at the behest of Moscow. Even in the later forties, after Romania's liberation, the communists were infinitely more concerned with consolidation of Soviet power and with their own political survival than with industrialization and modernization. If anything, industrialization was viewed as a political rather than an economic necessity, as the means of achieving the anti-rural and anti-bourgeois revolution, as an expression of the class struggle directed against "bourgeois-landlords" and other counterrevolutionary forces. It would be hard to prove, for instance, that the construction of the Danube-Black Sea Canal, a would-be monument to communist modernization, was undertaken for economic reasons.

Industrialization, even as it gathered momentum following the adoption of economic planning in the late forties, remained a function of Soviet and Romanian communist politics at least until the late fifties when it became a function of Romanian politics alone. This is to say that the emphasis placed on industrialization by Gheorghe Gheorghiu-Dej at the celebrated Plenum of November 1958 was an essential instrumentality for securing Gheorghiu's position in the incipient power struggle between Bucharest and Moscow. To survive the challenge posed to his authority and legitimacy by Khrushchev, the Romanian leader became the exponent of the doctrine of a "Romanian road to socialism" which entailed revival of the political slogan of pre-communist Romanian leaders *"Prin noi insine!"* ("By ourselves!") Romania was to concentrate on modernization within the objective historic conditions of the fifties - they, themselves, a function of the entire historic tradition of the Romanians - that is, within the confines of the Romanian national state, by Romanians, and for the ultimate benefit of Romanians.

In that manner, Gheorghiu-Dej and the Romanian communists hoped to emancipate themselves, as best they could, from total dependence on Moscow and the Soviet bloc and to reestablish economic, cultural, and even political ties with countries outside the Soviet orbit. Industrialization was chosen as a primary vehicle for attainment of political goals because communism presupposes industrialization and thus could not be regarded as deviationist or politically subversive action by Gheorghiu's enemies in the Kremlin. And, as the rift between Bucharest and Moscow widened in the early sixties, as Moscow opposed Romania's industrialization beyond the prescriptions of COMECON, Gheorghiu-Dej increasingly became intent on emphasizing the need for multilateral industrialization as the ultimate guarantee of national security and the ultimate expression of national goals and resolve. It was not until Ceausescu succeeded Gheorghiu-Dej in 1965, however, that multilateral industrialization became the ultimate purpose of the Romanian leadership.

Ceausescu's commitment to industrialization was directly and intimately related to the elemental political motive of survival. To secure and legitimize his power in the face of internal challenges and, particularly, of the Kremlin's opposition to Romania's independent course, Ceausescu opted for a political platform based on nationalism, communism, and modernization. He donned the mantle of executor of Romania's historic tradition which, according to him, called for the establishment of a multilaterally-developed national Romanian communist state ruled by an historic figure akin to that of great Romanian national leaders of the past - of men such as Stephen the Great or Michael the Brave - that of Nicolae Ceausescu. When Mary Ellen Fischer discusses the "cult" of Ceausescu in

Chapter 4, the effort by Romania's current leader to grasp legitimacy from images becomes all the more evident. Therefore, industrialization and the corollary creation of a communist society proceeded with a vengeance after 1965. However, because of the eminently political character of all of Ceausescu's actions, the grandiose schemes enunciated in successive plans for economic development have tended to ignore economic realities.

The rapid industrialization of Romania was unrelated to availability of capital, markets, or raw materials, to labor productivity, quality of production, or modern technology, with the result that by the beginning of the 1980s Ceausescu's grandiose plans are in jeopardy. Although industrialization proceeds apace, the strains on the agricultural sector are mounting since agricultural exports have become the primary source of the foreign capital required for continuing industrialization with resultant food shortages and growing social discontent. Disassociation from COMECON, within the limits of the prudent, is becoming less and less realizable because of growing dependence on Soviet oil and, from an economic standpoint, the outlook for further industrialization may become a function of factors related to the economic development of the Third World and of the industrial West. From a non-economic standpoint, however, Ceausescu's plans for the achievement of a multilaterally-developed Romanian communist society have thus far been more successful.

If the purpose of his drive for rapid industrialization was to secure political survival and aggrandizement, or perhaps to establish a Ceausescu dynasty, headed by Nicolae Ceausescu and his wife Elena, then the problems mentioned above may be overcome, at least in the short run, by skillful political maneuvering. It seems evident that the invocation of the Russian threat has been used since 1965 as the rationale for transforming the rather obscure Nicolae Ceausescu into the *defensor patriae* and protector of the historic interests of the Romanian people. The Czechoslovak crisis of 1968, during which Ceausescu announced Romania's determination to resist a possible Soviet invasion by force of arms, provided the basis for reinforcing the image of Ceausescu as the ultimate defender of Romanian interests and historic goals. Whether the Soviet threat was as grave as depicted by Ceausescu or whether techniques identified with "Peter and the Wolf" were used primarily to consolidate and expand his personal power, Ceausescu's political philosophy and actions have been, nevertheless, based on the assumption that he alone could secure Romania's future and safeguard and complete his own definition of the national historic tradition. That the Kremlin would have preferred different leaders in Romania is certain. But it is evident that Ceausescu's plans for securing his place in history transcended the threat of Soviet intervention. To the credit of this politically ambitious and intelligent man, as well as to that of his perhaps even more ambitious and intelligent wife, he has been able to diagnose and exploit the objective conditions which would insure attainment of his goals.

Ceausescu's foremost skills were revealed in his understanding and exploitation of international problems. He has skillfully exploited conflicts and contradictions involving China, the USSR, and the United States with a view to avoiding Soviet "intervention in Romania's internal affairs." Particularly important has been the prevention of maneuvers by Warsaw Pact forces on Romanian soil which, Ceausescu feared, would have erased the advantages gained in 1958 by the withdrawal of Soviet troops stationed in Romania. This partial disassociation from the Warsaw Pact, to which Walter Bacon refers in relationship to Romania's military policy, became a cardinal component of Ceausescu's doctrine of dissolution of military blocs in Europe after the invasion of Czechoslovakia. Romanian forces had failed to participate in the military actions directed by Warsaw Pact forces against Czechoslovakia. But in Ceausescu's estimate, protection against Soviet pressures had to transcend exploitation of the Sino-Soviet, Sino-American, and Soviet-American conflicts.

Thus, after 1968, Romanian foreign policy became all-encompassing through the gradual expansion of diplomatic and economic ties with Western Europe, Africa, Asia, Latin America, Israel, the Arab World, and almost every nation in the world. Such activism, which Ron Linden discusses more fully in Chapter 8, was all undertaken ostensibly for the purposes of securing world peace and acceptance, on a global basis, of Romania's principles regarding the rights of individual nations to pursue their own policies, external and internal, freely and without interference from the outside. But in another view, Romanian foreign policy was designed to establish Ceausescu as the arbiter of international conflicts and disputes involving the communist and non-communist worlds, to secure economic advantages for the developing Romanian industry, and ultimately to secure Ceausescu's position vis-a-vis the Kremlin by making implementation of the Brezhnev Doctrine in Romania if not impossible, at least very risky for the Soviet Union. There can be little doubt that that policy proved to be successful until the latter 1970s. For instance, Romania was instrumental in facilitating contacts between China and the United States in the late sixties and early seventies and between Egypt and Israel in the seventies. Romania has also established extensive economic and political ties with the Third World and has often taken stands different from those of other members of the Warsaw Pact in such delicate issues as the Arab-Israeli conflict or the Soviet invasion of Afghanistan (positions discussed more thoroughly by Linden's chapter).

Nevertheless, following the end of the Vietnamese war and the subsequent Sino-American rapprochement, the reorientation of American and Soviet foreign policies during the years of the Carter presidency, and the general international turmoil caused by the energy crisis and corollary problems in the Near and Middle East, Romania's importance in international affairs has declined considerably by the beginning of the 1980s. Whatever advantages Ceausescu may have obtained vis-a-vis the Soviet Union and on behalf of his own plans for Romania's development and for securing his place in contemporary and historic Romania through the pursuit of an ingenious foreign policy are apparently dissipating. In fact, it is improbable that Romania will be able to disassociate herself from active participation in Warsaw Pact, or even COMECON, affairs in the 1980s. Consequently, Ceausescu's security is likely to become more and more a function of his ability to defend his position of undisputed historic descendant of great Romanian leaders of the past and exclusive and indispensable champion and executor of Romania's communist destiny.

In these respects, Ceausescu's position appears quite secure at the beginning of the 1980s if, for no other reason, than that he has consolidated all power in his own hands and in those of his immediate personal and political families. It has long been argued that there are marked inconsistencies between Romania's enlightened foreign and Stalinist internal policies. The standard explanation for this dichotomy has been the need for maintenance of a domestic order acceptable to Moscow as a *quid pro quo* for Russian tolerance of Romanian deviations in foreign affairs. Thus, it has been said that as long as Ceausescu appeared to be more Stalinist than Brezhnev, the dreaded Brezhnev Doctrine could not be enforced against Romania. For supporters of that theory, the recent harsh attacks directed by Ceausescu against the independent Polish trade union movement merely reflect necessity and not conviction. Nothing could be further removed from the truth.

The history of internal political developments in Romania reveals that Ceausescu, as well as his immediate predecessor Gheorghiu-Dej, has always had authoritarian, Stalinist, or neo-Stalinist, views on the conduct of Romanian affairs. The reasons are fairly elementary. Gheorghiu-Dej was indeed more Stalinist than Stalin and had to be so to secure his own position in Stalin's days and later in those of Khrushchev. The beginnings of the Romanian road to independence, via a Romanian road to socialism, may indeed be traced to Khrushchev's determination to replace Gheorghiu-Dej in the period immediately following Khrushchev's de-Stalinization campaign. When, in 1957, Romanian supporters of Khrushchev sought to remove Gheorghiu-Dej from power following the elimination of the "anti-Party group" in Moscow by Khrushchev's forces, Gheorghiu-Dej purged the Khrushchevites and reinforced his campaign to build a Romanian road to socialism on neo-Stalinist lines, opposed to Khrushchevite innovations. However, as Romania's development by the early sixties required the development of meaningful economic and political ties with the capitalist West, the dangers of potential Soviet intervention and the spreading of "bourgeois" Western ideas into Romania proper became apparent to the Romanian communist leadership. Thus, such gestures of "liberalization" as were made by Gheorghiu-Dej prior to his death were reflective of the need to alleviate Western concerns rather than of fundamental changes in the character of his rule. And the limits of "liberalization" became more clearly defined during the early years of Ceausescu's rule.

Ceausescu's early "liberalism" was characteristic of transition periods. As Ceausescu succeeded to power at a time of rising, if cautious, expectations in Romania as well as one of transition from Khrushchev to Brezhnev in the USSR, he moved carefully. Nevertheless, certain characteristics of his future rule became evident from as early as 1965 when he assumed the roles of defender of Romania's national and historic interests in his relations with the USSR and of executor of the Romanian historic tradition, equated with the proximate establishment of a communist Romania. He was soon to become a communist *domnitor* (ruling prince) who would identify his rule with that of Michael the Brave, the Romanian hero of the late sixteenth century. Within a few short years, the self-styled defender and promoter of Romania's historic interests redefined the character of the rule of Michael the Brave from "patriotic" to "authoritarian." The transition occurred only at the beginning of the seventies chiefly because of the opportunities afforded by the Czechoslovak, and corollary Romanian crises of 1968. In 1968, Ceausescu acted like Michael the Brave in asserting his determination to lead the Romanian people in defense of the national patrimony and honor against foreign enemies. If Ceausescu the Savior did not become Ceausescu the Prince until 1971, it was because of continuing apprehension over Soviet intentions in the aftermath of the Czechoslovak crisis and the corollary need of securing Western support at a time of global reaction to the Soviet invasion of Czechoslovakia. President Nixon's visit to Romania, in the summer of 1969, coupled with Ceausescu's intense diplomatic activity in the name of international peace and of the rights of small nations greatly facilitated the consolidation of his power as a Romanian national hero. By 1971, the national hero was to become an absolute monarch. The genuine leadership of 1968, as Mary Ellen Fischer points out in her contribution, was not carried far into the 1970s, and now Ceausescu relies on images to preserve legitimacy.

It has been suggested that the turn to the left, directed against intellectuals, professional cadres, party leaders, and other individuals whose ideological purity and commitment to the rapid development of the multilaterally-developed national communist state was questioned in 1971, was adopted because of Ceausescu's admiration for the Chinese cultural revolution and continued fears over Soviet hostility toward his rule. It seems doubtful, however, that the Romanian cultural revolution of the seventies was an offspring of the Chinese and it is also questionable whether continuing Soviet hostility was a determining factor in the termination of the "liberal" phase of Ceausescu's rule. It is also possible that Ceausescu's plans for multilateral development could not have been achieved without the establishment of rigid party discipline and centralized control. It may also be true that Soviet pressure, exercised through military maneuvers, disputes over the legitimacy of the acquisition of Bessarabia in 1940, and encouragement of the aspirations of the dissatisfied Hungarian minority in Transylvania, may have contributed to Ceausescu's actions. However, in the last analysis, the turn to the left must be attributed to Ceausescu's determination to secure total power at the first available opportunity. By invoking the need for national unity, discipline, defense of the national patrimony, and modernization at a time when the gradual consolidation of power in his own hands and in those of his family had run its course, Ceausescu merely completed the traditional political cycle of Romanian rulers, communist or not, whereby security and power are guaranteed only by absolute rule. And indeed, Ceausescu's quest for power and security assumed, by the late seventies, the most accomplished forms of personal rule characterized by the most elaborate manifestations of a cult of personality unrivaled since the days of Stalin and Mao Tse-tung.

As the absolute ruler of Romania, Ceausescu has appropriated the traditional slogan of previous monarchs "Orthodoxy, Autocracy,

Nationality," albeit within the context and objective conditions of the contemporary Romanian state. "Orthodoxy" presupposes enforcement of a nationalist, neo-Marxist ideology, formulated by Ceausescu and his close associates. Its essence consists of identification of the historic tradition and goals of the Romanians with communism and corollary rejection of all other possible interpretations of the Romanians' manifest destiny. Orthodoxy is by definition dogmatic and anti-intellectual. It tolerates no deviations from Ceausescu's pronunciamentos on matters ideological and requires constant reiteration of the official dogma in all media of intellectual expression. (Trond Gilberg's chapter in this volume considers, at length, the regime's socialization efforts.) Adulation of the leader and of his thoughts is a prerequisite for any and all Romanians and any form of dissent has become impardonable.

"Autocracy" has the simple meaning of total acceptance of one-man rule and of recognition of the infallibility of that man's actions and decisions. All power belongs to Ceausescu who rules with the assistance of the traditionally supportive spouse and members of the "king's household."

"Nationality" means rule by the Romanian majority and imposition of the Romanians' historic tradition on national minorities with a view to creating a Romanian national communist state. Internationalism is acceptable only as an expression of Romanian national interests and cosmopolitanism is rejected altogether.

The rigid enforcement of these cardinal principles of Ceausescu's dogma has increased the resentment toward the Ceausescu dynasty, as Dan Nelson suggests, among the working class, but has not threatened the security of that dynasty. The enforcement of the principles identified with Orthodoxy has harmed the intellectual and professional community but has had apparently little effect on the masses in general. The incessant calls for ideological purity and imposition of Ceausescu's ideological positions have had their most negative effects on the educational system, on writers of Romanian history, on writers and artists in general, on technocrats and scientists, on physicians, and on all thinking individuals who are aware of the motivations of the leaders and the emptiness of the official dogma. However, despite disaffection and despair, the majority of those exposed to and affected by the imposition of dogmatic communist orthodoxy are paying at least lip service to Ceausescu's line mostly because the opportunities for defection abroad have declined considerably in recent years. On the other hand, Ceausescu's dogmatism has won him the support of opportunists and of those elements of the population who stand to benefit from his anti-intellectualism, anti-cosmopolitanism, and acerbic nationalism. Advancement in the professions has become easier for the faithful and the incompetent both because of the leader's lack of confidence in cosmopolitan, bourgeois or *embourgeoisé*, intellectual or neo-intellectual professional cadres and of the vacancies created by the loss of such cadres through emigration or defection abroad. Moreover, Ceausescu's determination to consolidate his power as the executor of the Romanian masses' historic aspirations has resulted in the broadening of the nominal participation of the masses in political life through the enormous enlargement of the size of the Romanian Communist Party. Indeed, through the deliberate political socialization, discussed by Gilberg, the Party has become a mass organization and the privileges bestowed upon its members have tended to secure the power of the rulers and the interests of the privileged groups in the Romanian communist state.

For these reasons, too, there has been wider popular acceptance, or at least toleration, of autocracy and the corollary deification of Ceausescu than critics would like to have us believe. Since autocracy is ostensibly necessary to defend the historic interests of Romanians, primarily against the Soviet Union, the Romanian masses generally subscribe to the view that Ceausescu can best defend Romania's independence. And even his critics, mostly intellectuals, students, and national minorities who rightly ridicule the identification of Ceausescu with historic figures in the past such as Burebista, Vlad the Impaler, Stephen the Great, Michael the Brave, and others who are aware of the fact that Ceausescu's autocracy is designed primarily to build "socialism within one family," still believe that Ceausescu is preferable to Brezhnev. That Ceausescu's internal policies are regarded as faulty, if not disastrous, from an economic point of view by the majority of the population, does not mean that the same public, desiring Hungarian-style reforms, has any evident alternatives to Ceausescu's rule at this time.

The most notable exception to this attitude is found among the immobile national minorities, specifically the Hungarians. Whereas Jews and Saxons have been able to leave Romania during the last fifteen years or so, the immobile Hungarians have been growing impatient with the Ceausescu regime in recent years. The alleged reason for the Hungarian's discontent is the adoption of Romanization policies detrimental to their constitutional and historic rights. The enforcement of the principle of "Nationality" has indeed affected the Hungarian minority more than any other. In theory, Ceausescu has abided by the letter of the constitution and implemented laws whereby the rights of national minorities are guaranteed. In practice, however, pressure has been intensified during the last decade for at least cultural assimilation through gradual reduction in the number of Hungarian-language schools and opportunities for professional advancement of unintegrated or unassimilated Hungarians. Moreover, the Hungarians have been resentful of the Romanization of urban centers inhabited primarily by Hungarians which has involved the Romanization of street names, resettlement of Romanians from provinces other than Transylvania into enlarged industrial towns, and a general dismemberment of Hungarian urban values and traditions. And indeed, the rapid transformation of the historic character of Transylvania has been a deliberate policy of Ceausescu even though it is not necessarily directed against the Hungarians alone. In fact, the Romanization of Transylvanian towns has been motivated primarily by the ruler's determination to destroy bourgeois or *embourgeoise* urban centers and traditions throughout Romania through transformation of commercial towns into industrial ones with corollary relocation of the masses. These polices have affected most directly the Transylvanian urban centers, the historic foci of Hungarian and Saxon culture and civilization.

Ultimately, however, the resentment of the Hungarians is based on their awareness of the differences between economic, cultural, and political conditions in Hungary and Romania and to their lack of allegiance to the doctrines of Romanian historic rights and manifest destiny enunciated by Ceausescu. In itself, the Hungarians' dissatisfaction is not too significant to the rulers of Romania. It assumes significance, however, in terms of its exploitation by the Kremlin and by Budapest as a means for potential interference in Romanian internal affairs. And it is this ultimate concern of Ceausescu for the security of his regime that brings us to the final assessment of Romania's status at the beginning of the 1980s and likely evolution of Ceausescu's Romania during the rest of that decade.

As the possibility of direct Soviet military intervention in Romania appears increasingly remote in view of Ceausescu's decreased opportunities for pursuing policies of genuine independence from Moscow, the gradual erosion of Ceausescu's legitimacy and power as leader of an independent national communist state appears inevitable. During the 1980s Romania is likely to become ever more dependent on the Soviet Union for attainment of her economic goals. In all likelihood, Ceausescu will continue to seek alternatives to greater reliance on the USSR and COMECON; yet the chances of securing continuing economic support from the West and the

Third World at the levels required by the ambitious plans for multilateral development appear illusory. Increased dependence on Moscow is bound to devalue one of Ceausescu's main trump cards - resistance to Soviet interference in Romanian affairs. It is also not likely to offer solutions to Romania's precarious economic conditions. As it is improbable that the Romanian leadership will abandon its grandiose plans for development, growing disenchantment with the Ceausescu regime by a discontented Romanian population will probably constitute the primary threat to Ceausescu's political survival in the eighties. Dan Nelson's contribution, for example, provides evidence of such a trend.

The 1980s are also likely to witness a further decline in Ceausescu's role as world leader. As Western Europe appears eager to seek long-range accommodation with Moscow, as the need for intermediaries between the Great Powers and the Third World diminishes, as America's relations with China stabilize and develop, the unique diplomatic opportunities grasped by Ceausescu during the sixties and seventies are not likely to recur. In all probability, Ceausescu will assume the position of just another leader of a communist country whose services may be used for tactical rather than for strategic purposes by interested parties, big or small.

The diminution of Ceausescu's importance in international affairs is also likely to contribute to exacerbation of Romania's internal problems. In the absence of any compelling need to overlook or justify the rigidity of Ceausescu's domestic polices by virtue of their being either required for the survival of his regime or excusable because of his great contributions to world peace, those policies are bound to be subject to harsher criticism by the West and by "dissidents" both at home and abroad. Thus, as the indispensable man will become increasingly less essential to more and more of his present supporters, it is probable that Ceausescu's star will dim in the near future. By the end of the 1980s he would be 71 years old; he may very well not be celebrating his seventieth birthday as President of the Socialist Republic of Romania or as General Secretary of the Romanian Communist Party.

Romania's development as a communist state is predictable only for the duration of Ceausescu's rule. The circumstances of the termination of that rule are a matter of conjecture. They will, however, determine the further evolution of Romania whenever they will occur. And the ensuing changes should be drastic.

CHAPTER FIVE

MARXIST THOUGHT AND THE RISE OF NATIONALISM

In a vain attempt to seek ideological connections between Marxism and nationalism, communist ideologues are trying to find organic and converging links between these two incompatible and, in fact, mutually exclusive ideologies. In the process they have simplified, and also distorted, the essential characteristics of Marxism and of nationalism to suit their officially-mandated theories.[1]

This is not to say that the reconciliation of Marxism and nationalism is not impossible on the terms chosen by East European political leaders and the articulators and propagators of their basic political views - the historians. In essence, contemporary East European nationalism and Marxism share the common denominators of anti-imperialism, social revolution, and attainment of the alleged ultimate goal of all inhabitants of the countries of Eastern Europe - communism. Thus, since a correct, or at least meaningful, reconciliation of Marxist ideology and nationalism is impossible, the required legitimacy of Marxist ideology has been translated into a mythical historical theory which has little, if anything, in common with either Marxism or the actual history of Eastern Europe.[2]

What, after all, is the true essence of historic East European nationalism? Basically, it is the attainment of the presumed goal of the peoples of Eastern Europe of national statehood and independence from foreign domination. In other words, it is an expression of anti-imperialism.[3] It is true that in certain instances East European nationalism was directed against the defunct Habsburg and Ottoman empires and that the so-called struggle for national liberation was aided or abetted by the Russian empire. Indeed, Czech, Slovak, and Bulgarian nationalisms have had close links with the "Big Slavic Brother" from the East. However, this was untrue of Romanian and Polish nationalisms, for instance, which have been largely expressions of anti-Russianism. There can be little doubt that the triumph of Russian imperialism at the end of World War II did not endear the rulers of the Kremlin and their representatives in early postwar Eastern Europe to the politically-active, or even passive, inhabitants of the national states of that part of Europe. The Soviet empire was intolerable on nationalist grounds.[4] It was illegitimate because Marxism was an alien, non-Christian ideology whereas East European nationalism was expressly and intimately related to and legitimized by Christianity and its representatives, spiritual and secular. It was unacceptable because it repudiated the ultimate achievement of the successful national struggle, the transformation - albeit often incomplete - of the peasantry into a property-owing petite-bourgeoisie. It was despised because the enforcers of the new imperialist order were mostly Jews.[5]

One may well ask what is the essence of East European Marxism? Here, of course, the answers vary.[6] However, whether Marxist ideology was enunciated by Hungarian intellectuals, Polish labor leaders, Yugoslav theorists, or Romanian apparatchiks, it parroted during the early postwar years the anti-nationalist, Stalinist, Marxist utterances which were totally incompatible with the historic traditions of the nation states of Eastern Europe. In fact, it is fair to say that East European Marxism, then, and in most instances even now, is an ideology which legitimizes "socialist transformation" according to the blueprints developed in, or at least compatible with the interests of, the Soviet Union for the express purpose of legitimizing the power and policies of the communist rulers of Eastern Europe. It is not surprising, therefore, that the Marxist doctrine of proletarian internationalism was given precedence over inappropriate evocations of Marx's eloquent and repeated advocacy of Polish independence from, or of Romanian rights vis-a-vis, Russian imperialism.[7]

The reconciliation of Marxist ideology and historic nationalism in Eastern Europe has thus been artificial, and in the process Marxism suffered more than nationalism.

The initial impetus for the revival of nationalism in Eastern Europe came from Stalin himself when the purging of Jewish leaders such as Rudolf Slansky and Ana Pauker took place either on the initiative of the Kremlin or with its approval.[8] Anti-Semitism, the lowest common denominator of nationalism in Eastern Europe, was designed to defuse the anti-Russianism of the Stalinist period in an effort to seek mass identification with an ethnically authochtonous - albeit Stalinist - leadership. Ethnic purification as such could not be regarded as incompatible with Marxist ideology since the new communist leaders failed to enunciate doctrines at variance with proletarian internationalism, national equality, or Marx's preference for large political units. However, even before Stalin's death, Tito's heretical positions on individual roads to socialism facilitated the formulation, still in very tentative and cautious terms, of the hybrid and ideologically-suspect neo-nationalist doctrine of "socialist patriotism."[9] The "road to socialist patriotism," as it evolved between 1948 and its full-fledged formulation in the early years of the Khrushchev era, was one winding from proletarian internationalism, through proletarian patriotism, to socialist patriotism. However, no matter what ideological sophistry and euphemisms may have been used in Eastern Europe in the years antedating the Polish and Hungarian crises of 1956, socialist patriotism, to be palatable to the masses, had to contain two essential ingredients - anti-Stalinism and anti-Semitism.

In a sense, socialist patriotism proved to be a moderating force in 1956 as it allowed the venting of anti-Stalinism and anti-Semitism of the Hungarian revolutionaries against the ostensibly unrepresentative "Judeo-communist" clique of Matyas Rakosi rather than against the moderate Khrushchevites, tolerant of socialist patriotism but opposed to bourgeois nationalism.[10] The installation of Janos Kadar as the presumed representative of the Hungarian communist tradition - allegedly moderate and rooted in the history of the Hungarian labor movement - however, led to the questionable equating of the historic evolution of Hungary with that of the history of Hungarian communism and to the validation of a broader doctrine of socialist patriotism as one representative of the historic aspirations of the Hungarian people.[11] What was true of Hungary was to be even truer of Poland when Wladislaw Gomulka was represented as the exponent of the historic Polish communist tradition, a tradition held compatible - if not necessarily identical - with the totality of the historic traditions of Poland.[12]

The convergence of the histories of the countries of Eastern Europe with those of the histories of the communist movements into socialist patriotism, however, could hardly be legitimized on Marxist ideological grounds. Nor was socialist patriotism justifiable on historic grounds since historic nationalism could not be divorced from anti-communism and, more often than not, anti-Russianism. Nevertheless, socialist patriotism of the Hungarian and Polish vintage was tolerable to the Kremlin because of its compatibility with proletarian internationalism and corollary subordination to Soviet political interests.

Less tolerable, from Khrushchev's standpoint, was the Romanian version of socialist patriotism which emerged in the early 1950s and which evolved, gradually, during the Khrushchev era into an essentially anti-Russian "nationalist-socialist" doctrine.[13] Romanian socialist patriotism was an extension of the confrontation between the ethnic Romanian and the non-Romanian, largely Jewish, segments of the Romanian Communist Party which resulted in the victory of the Romanian group headed by

Gheorghe Gheorghiu-Dej. Viewed harmless in its origins by Stalin, it was challenged by Khrushchev from as early as 1954 because of Gheorghiu-Dej's utilization of socialist patriotism as an instrument for the continuation in power of his Stalinist Romanian group which Khrushchev sought to remove. Gheorghiu-Dej's questioning of the legitimacy of a Russian military presence in Romania by virtue of the Red Armies' having liberated Romania in 1944 by claiming that Romania's liberation was achieved by the revolutionary actions of the Romanian communists themselves, his enunciation - albeit in a tentative manner - of the applicability of Tito's views on "independent roads to socialism" to Romania, and his overtures to Mao Tse-tung were recognized as anti-Soviet manifestations by Khrushchev who, however, had to tolerate them in the years of consolidation of power and crises which affected his leadership from 1954 to 1958.[14] The Romanians' support of the Soviet military intervention in Hungary in 1956, although welcomed by the Kremlin at that time, did not alleviate Khrushchev's suspicions of the purpose of Gheorghiu-Dej's socialist patriotism. In fact, the elimination of the Magyar Autonomous Region of Transylvania in the aftermath of the Hungarian revolution, justified by the Romanians in Marxist ideological terms as compatible with the assimilation of small nations and with Soviet practices regarding national minorities, was clearly an attempt by Gheorghiu-Dej to secure his own position by rallying the traditional anti-Magyar and anti-Semitic sentiments of the Romanians on the side of actions which he proclaimed to be compatible with the historic interests of all Romanians and with those of the Romanian Communist Party as well. By 1958, Romanian-styled socialist patriotism assumed yet another dimension, unacceptable to Moscow, as Gheorghiu-Dej removed all Khrushchevites from power, engaged in a massive Romanianization of the cadres, secured the removal of the Soviet armed forces from Romania through a squeeze play involving the People's Republic of China and Khrushchev's need for "détente" with the West, and proclaimed the convergence of the Romanians' historic interests with those of the Romanian Communist Party into a common historic tradition. That tradition was both "patriotic" - a clear euphemism for nationalistic - and "socialist" and called for the development of "socialism within one Romanian state" under the leadership of the Romanian Communist Party.[15] By 1960, Romanian political leaders and historians were hard at work refining Gheorghiu-Dej's historic theories and, by 1964, they legitimized the "nationalizing" of socialist patriotism in both historic and Marxist terms. The historic rights of the

Romanians to political independence, to the securing of the historic boundaries of Greater Romania - which implied the regaining of Bessarabia from the Soviet Union - and to protecting their national interests against "interference in internal affairs" by external powers were expounded in a remarkable work, "Marx on the Romanians," in which Marx's condemnation of Russian imperialism and justification of Romania's road to independence and socialism were spelled out in no uncertain terms.[16]

This formulation of socialist patriotism, which revived territorial revisionism and bourgeois nationalism, was unacceptable to the Kremlin and was also rejected by all socialist states of Eastern Europe - with the exception of Albania and Yugoslavia - because it was anti-Soviet and, at least in the case of Hungary, it entailed discrimination against the Hungarian minority in Transylvania.

The changes in leadership in both Romania and the Soviet Union, with Ceausescu and Brezhnev replacing Gheorghiu-Dej and, respectively, Khrushchev, failed to lessen the growing hostility between Bucharest and Moscow; if anything, Ceausescu's socialist-nationalism became all the more strident between 1965 and 1968, and his constant references to Romania's historic rights to Bessarabia were met with increasingly greater displeasure by Brezhnev.[17]

Although it would be presumptuous to assume that the Romanian national-socialist course directly affected the evolution of events in Czechoslovakia that led to the removal of Antonin Novotny's clique and to the ensuing sequence of events which resulted in the Soviet intervention of August 1968, it is certain that Brezhnev's initial support of the reformers reflected the Kremlin's willingness to tolerate socialist patriotism as long as it did not deviate from the essential principles of proletarian internationalism and Marxism-Leninism.[18] Whether the military action of 1968 was prompted by fears that deviant socialist patriotism of the Czechoslovak or Romanian varieties presented a threat to the security of other socialist nations is still a matter of dispute. Certainly, however, the Czechoslovak variety was more dangerous to the leaders of the Soviet Union, the German Democratic Republic, Poland, and Bulgaria than the Romanian, although the military threats directed against Romania shortly after the invasion of Czechoslovakia reflected Brezhnev's desire to at least eliminate the anti-Russian elements of Ceausescu's version.[19]

Yet, socialist patriotism did not end after 1968; in fact, it was encouraged by the Soviet Union, for its own purposes, in all countries loyal to the Kremlin. However, the engineered and/or tolerated variants proved counterproductive in Poland, ineffectual as a deterrent to Ceausescu's and, because of unexpected side effects, detrimental to the interests of the Kremlin both politically and ideologically.

The "Brezhnev Doctrine," enunciated in 1968, required the retention of specific national identities and historic traditions to camouflage its neo-Stalinism at a time when détente was still advocated and national liberation movements and support of other nationalist causes remained an integral part of the struggle against "imperialism and Zionism." It was essential for the Kremlin to defuse not only anti-Soviet reaction within and outside the socialist camp but also to legitimize the intervention in ideological terms. "Socialism with a human face" was branded a heresy perpetrated by exponents of "bourgeois nationalism" and "cosmopolitanism" and denounced as an anti-Soviet manifestation, unrepresentative of the historic traditions of Czechoslovakia. According to Moscow, the Czechoslovak socialist patriotism of the Dubcek era was false socialist patriotism in that it betrayed the historic goals of the peoples of Czechoslovakia by deviating from the anti-German, anti-imperialist, and anti-Zionist traditions. On the other hand, correct socialist patriotism - anti-German, anti-Zionist, and anti-imperialist - patterned on Soviet "Marxist-Leninist" principles and practices was eminently desirable not only for Czechoslovakia but also for the rest of the loyal members of the socialist camp.[20]

The legitimizing of the communist regimes in Eastern Europe through history did not lower the levels of anti-Sovietism and anti-communism but did increase, in varying ways, the levels of nationalism of the peoples of Eastern Europe. The effects were least negative, from a Soviet standpoint, in Bulgaria where the national historic tradition had been intimately linked with that of Russia, at least since the nineteenth century, and the communist tradition with that of the Soviet Union, at least since the days of Lenin and Dimitrov. Still, the recognition of the paramount role played by the Orthodox Church in Bulgaria's liberation in 1878, the celebration of historic anniversaries such as that of 1,300 years since the establishment of the first Bulgarian state, and the renewing of such traditional controversial issues as the Macedonian Question have revived at least some of the fervor of Bulgarian nationalists, whether communists or not.[21]

In Czechoslovakia, despite the depiction of German imperialists as the historic enemies and the Russians as the historic friends of the peoples of Czechoslovakia and the obliteration of T. G. Masaryk's role in the formation of the Czechoslovak Republic, the renewed concern over Huss and Hussitism cannot help but engender different interpretations of the true Czechoslovak historic tradition than the official one which the neo-Stalinist regime of Gustav Husak has authorized for mass consumption.[22]

Even in the German Democratic Republic where socialist patriotism cannot have any historic context other than commitment to the anti-fascist and anti-imperialist struggle and allegiance to Marxism-Leninism, the rulers' ultimate historic goal of a united, socialist, "democratic" Germany has failed to persuade the majority of its inhabitants that the alternate western solution corresponds more closely to the realities of German history.[23]

In the less isolated or totally subservient client states, Hungary and Poland, socialist patriotism assumed different forms. In Hungary, history was "reinterpreted" more than falsified to demonstrate that the Hungarian masses have always been socialist by both instinct and nature. Anti-Germanism and anti-Zionism have been played down; the politically-sensitive Transylvanian question, however, has been reopened. In fact, the Transylvanian problem, focusing on the "anti-Marxist" violation of the Romanian regime of the rights of the Hungarian nationality of that province, has become a major weapon in Moscow's and, by extension, Budapest's determination to restrain, if not eliminate, the excesses of Romania's socialist-nationalism.[24]

The Polish variant, however, was to cause grave problems. Gomulka's replacement by Edward Gierek was not necessarily a concession to the bourgeois and anti-Soviet tendencies of the working masses, but it was an acknowledgment of the fact that the doctrine of convergence of the Polish communist tradition, as personified by Gomulka's team, and the Polish historic tradition was imperfect. That imperfection became increasingly more evident in the 1970s when even more meaningful attempts at reconciling the actual Polish historic tradition, identified in no small measure with the historic role of the Catholic Church and with both anti-Russianism and anti-Germanism, and the Polish communist tradition failed to forestall the political explosion of 1980. The forcible fusion of the two traditions into the uneasy Jaruzelski compromise, in which socialist patriotism is more historical and patriotic than that of the Czechoslovak, East German, or Bulgarian travesties, nevertheless appears to be at best an interim formulation of that doctrine.[25]

Romanian socialist patriotism alone has evolved along lines basically unacceptable to Brezhnev and his successors. After 1968 Ceausescu enunciated the doctrine of his being the executor of the Romanian historic tradition since the days of the anti-imperialist Dacian chieftain Burebista, which presupposes the attainment of communism within the historic borders of Romania and protection of the people's security against hostile actions by imperialists and revisionists.[26] As the champion of Romanianism, Ceausescu has also sought the support of the diaspora for the achievement of his historic mission. As a result, the Orthodox Church and national heroes of the past - all identified as promoters of Romanian national interests and fighters for independence - have been legitimized as essential components of Ceausescu's historic synthesis.[27]

The involvement of the diaspora has become an important factor in contemporary East European nationalism not only for the Romanian but, albeit for different reasons, also for the Hungarian and Polish regimes. In the case of the Romanians, neofascist elements have been incorporated into socialist nationalism since the anti-Russian and anti-Hungarian diaspora consists largely of former members or past or present sympathizers of the Iron Guard of whom many have accepted the leadership of anti-communist and anti-Semitic members of the clergy. In fact, were it not for the substitution of Marxism-Leninism for Orthodoxy, Ceausescu's socialist patriotism would be entirely compatible with the authoritarian nationalism of the Romanian "right."[28]

The Hungarian regime has also appealed to the diaspora not so much in an effort to heal the wounds inflicted upon Magyardom by the events of 1956 as to enlist its support in combatting Romanian actions directed against the Hungarian population of Transylvania. However, just as in the case of the Romanian diaspora, reconciliation of communist and anti-communist - often neofascist doctrines - has become necessary and, in the process, Hungarian socialist patriotism has been tainted. Indeed, it has to tolerate ideological and political positions reminiscent of the Horthy era which are intrinsically anti-communist, often anti-Semitic, and usually embarrassing since the diaspora's territorial revisionism normally includes not only Transylvania but also Hungarian lands taken by the Soviet Union at the end of World War II.[29]

The Polish search for support from the diaspora, whether by *Solidarity* or by Jaruzelski's regime, is too well known to require much comment. Both sides have encountered problems similar to those which have faced the Romanians and the Hungarians and the uneasy compromise between the Party, the people, and the Catholic Church in Poland reflects the importance of the participation of the diaspora in the stabilization of the national socialist Polish state.[30]

All this is to say that East European nationalism is alive, and well, and living not only in Warsaw, Bucharest, Budapest, Sofia and Bratislava, but also in Chicago, Detroit, Cleveland, Paris, London, Munich, Madrid, Buenos Aires, and other places which the length of this paper prevents from being enumerated.[31] As such, contemporary East European nationalism, with the partial exception of the Romanian and, to a lesser extent, the Polish, is largely a function of Soviet political goals and interests. It cannot subvert the communist order in Eastern Europe but it can, to a limited degree, reinforce the power - if not the legitimacy - of the various heads of governments and parties of the socialist camp. Although ever-more-remote from Marxist ideology and even from the limits to which socialist patriotism was originally acceptable to the Kremlin, it continues to serve the interests of the Soviet Union or of the national communist leaders themselves. The "left-wing fascist" tendencies of Ceausescu's nationalism can be condoned by Moscow because his "Peronism" can be used to advantage in the Kremlin's relations with Khadafi and other left-wing fascists of the Third World.[32] Economic considerations outweigh the potentially negative consequences of Jaruzelski's flirtations with anti-communists in the diaspora and the imperialist camp. Kadar's contacts with Horthyites and "Fifty-sixers" cannot be faulted as long as they contribute to the Kremlin's policies of divide-and-conquer. Zhivkov's enrollment of the Orthodox Church in the Macedonian Question is permissible as long as it embarrasses the post-Titoist regime in Yugoslavia.[33] Even Enver Hoxha's agitation in Kosova is tolerable for the same reasons.[34] Anti-Zionism, equatable with anti-Semitism rather than with Marxism, is essential for Soviet-Arab relations and had best been mastered by East European nationalists long before Stalin. At the same time, however, the involvement of the diasporas and the contamination of socialist patriotism with traditional historic components of East European nationalism is counterproductive in that the diasporas are most powerful in the United States, Canada, Germany, France, and South America and since in every instance, they are distinctly anti-communist. The diasporas, therefore, tend to identify themselves most readily with conservative, anti-communist regimes not least of which is that of President Reagan. Probably for that reason, the largely anti-communist inhabitants of Eastern Europe, who are most supportive of Reagan's foreign policies, favor official contacts with co-nationals in the western world. Thus, the expansion of socialist patriotism entails certain risks for the Kremlin and for the leaders of Eastern Europe which may, at some time in the future, outweigh the advantages of using nationalism for their own political purposes.

ENDNOTES

1. A stimulating, far-reaching discussion of these issues is contained in a symposium on "Left-Wing Fascism," *Society*, XVIII:4 (1981), pp. 19-40. See also the important articles contained in a special issue on "East Central Europe: Continuity and Change" of the *Journal of International Affairs*, XX:1 (1966), especially "East Central Europe: Continuity and Change" by Stephen Fischer-Galati, pp. 1-8 and "Nationalism and National Minorities in Eastern Europe" by Thomas T. Hammond, p. 9-31.

2. Several articles on myths in East European history are contained in *East European Quarterly*, XV:3 (1981), pp. 307-355. Of particular interest is George Barany, "On Truth in Myths," pp. 347-355.

3. A penetrating analysis and interpretation of East European nationalism in the historic and contemporary perspectives will be found in Franjo Tudjman, *Nationalism in Contemporary Europe* (Boulder and New York: East European Monographs, 1981), especially parts I, III, IV, and V.

4. The most incisive and stimulating analysis of historic East European nationalism in the historic perspective remains Hugh Seton-Watson, *Eastern Europe Between the Wars* (Cambridge: Cambridge University Press, 1945). The detailed, perceptive, *Nationalism in Eastern Europe* (Seattle: University of Washington Press, 1969), with contributions by the editors of the volume, Peter F. Sugar and Ivo Lederer, and other specialists, is essential for the study of East European nationalism. Stimulating, if somewhat controversial, is also Robin Okey, *Eastern Europe 1740-1980: Feudalism to Communism* (Minneapolis: University of Minnesota Press, 1982), especially chapters 3, 9, and 10.

5. Interesting and original contributions to these issues are contained in Bela Vago and George L. Mosse (eds.), *Jews and non-Jews in Eastern Europe* (New York, Toronto: John Wiley & Sons, 1974) and in Bela Vago (ed.), *Jewish Assimilation in Modern Times* (Boulder: Westview Press, 1981).

6. The most valuable information on this subject is to be found in Francois Fejto, *History of the People's Democracies* (London: Pelican, 1973).

7. Of great significance in this respect is *K. Marx - Insemnari despre romani* (K. Marx's Notes on the Romanians), ed. by A. Otetea and S. Schwann (Bucharest: Editura Academiei, 1964).

8. Interesting interpretations are to be found in Stephen Fischer-Galati (ed.), *Eastern Europe in the Sixties* (New York: Praeger, 1963).

9. A good survey is by H. Gordon Skilling, "National Communism in Eastern Europe," *The Canadian Journal of Economics and Political Science*, XXX:3, 1964, pp. 313-327.

10. On Rakosi see especially Bennett Kovrig, *The Hungarian People's Republic* (Baltimore: The Johns Hopkins Press, 1970), pp. 97-110.

11. On these problems consult the monumental *The First War Between Socialist States: The Hungarian Revolution of 1956 and its Impact* (New York: Brooklyn College Press, 1984), ed. by Bela K. Kiraly, Barbara Lotze, and Nandor F. Dreisziger, especially parts I-IV.

12. See especially M. K. Dziewanowski, *The Communist Party of Poland* (Cambridge: Harvard University Press, 1976), pp. 267-311 and Michael Checinski, *Poland: Communism, Nationalism, Anti-Semitism* (New York: Karz-Cohl), pp. 104-145.

13. Stephen Fischer-Galati, *The New Rumania: From People's Democracy to Socialist Republic* (Cambridge: The M.I.T. Press, 1967), pp. 44-77.

14. Ibid.

15. Stephen Fischer-Galati, *Twentieth Century Rumania* (New York: Columbia University Press, 1970), pp. 128-158.

16. See note 7, above. See also Fischer-Galati, *The New Rumania*, pp. 100 ff. and William E. Griffith, *Sino-Soviet Relations, 1964-1965* (Cambridge: The M.I.T. Press, 1967), pp. 269-296.

17. Fischer-Galati, *Twentieth Century Rumania*, pp. 183-210.

18. See the various pertinent documents contained in Robin A. Remington, *Winter in Prague: Documents on Czechoslovak Communism in Crisis* (Cambridge: The M.I.T. Press, 1969).

19. A series of interesting and relevant studies on the Romanian issues are contained in Daniel N. Nelson (ed.), *Romania in the 1980s* (Boulder: Westview Press, 1981).

20. An introspective analysis of these issues will be found in the readable volume by Zdenek Krystufek, *The Soviet Regime in Czechoslovakia* (Boulder and New York: East European Monographs, 1981), pp. 144-197.

21. An interesting study on Bulgarian communism in this context is by L.A.D. Dellin, "The Communist Party of Bulgaria" in Stephen Fischer-Galati (ed.), *The Communist Parties of Eastern Europe* (New York: Columbia University Press, 1979), pp. 49-85. See also the remarkable "diary in letters" by the Bulgarian-Macedonian writer Venko Markovski, *Goli Otok: The Island of Death* (Boulder and New York: Social Science Monographs, 1984).

22. Interesting observations are to be found in Joseph Held, "Cultural Development" in Stephen Fischer-Galati (ed.), *Eastern Europe in the 1980s* (Boulder: Westview Press, 1981), pp. 257-278.

23. Ibid.

24. On the endless Transylvanian polemics see the periodical *Carpathian Observer* and other like publications which echo the essential views of all parties concerned.

25. On Polish problems see the latest major work by Adam Bromke, *Eastern Europe in the Aftermath of Solidarity* (Boulder and New York: East European Monographs, 1985).

26. Stephen Fischer-Galati, "Myths in Romanian History," *East European Quarterly*, XV:3 (1981), pp. 327-334.

27. Stephen Fischer-Galati, "'Autocracy, Orthodoxy, Nationality' in the Twentieth Century: The Romanian Case," *East European Quarterly*, XVIII:1 (1984), pp. 25-34.

28. Ibid.

29. Much is to be gained by reading contributions in John F. Cadzow, Andrew Ludanyi, and Louis J. Elteto, *Transylvania: The Roots of Ethnic Conflict* (Kent: The Kent State University Press, 1983).

30. Interesting materials are contained in Donald E. Pienkos, *PNA: A Centennial History of the Polish National Alliance of the United States of America* (Boulder and New York: East European Monographs, 1984).

31. "Left-Wing Fascism," *Society*, XVIII:4 (1981), pp. 30-31.

32. Ibid.

33. See note 21, above.

34. The varying views on Kosova, representative of differing national interests, are represented in *Studies on Kosova* (Boulder and New York: East European Monographs, 1984), edited by Arshi Pipa and Sami Repishti and in Alex N. Dragnich and Slavko Todorovich, *The Saga of Kosovo: Focus on Serbian-Albanian Relations* (Boulder and New York: East European Monographs, 1984).

CHAPTER SIX

THE "TAKEOVER" IN THE HISTORIC PERSPECTIVE

The "revolutionary" events of 1989 and the corollary repudiation of communism have led many students of East European developments since the "Takeover" to reinterpret the history and political culture of the countries of Eastern Europe. The dominant view would make us believe that the "Takeover" itself and the ensuing communist period were an aberration from the democratic traditions and politics of Eastern Europe. Of course, the definition of democratic traditions and concepts varies considerably in function of the political ideologies and interests of the exponents of such theories.

Speakers for "bourgeois democracy" extol the activities and philosophies of liberal bourgeois, socialist, and peasant political parties even though the achievements and constituencies of those organizations do not necessarily correspond to the image created by their contemporary champions. The more vocal spokesmen for "populist democracy" reject the claims of bourgeois democratic forces as distorted and self-serving; instead, they suggest that "fascism" or variations thereof were in consort with the political culture of the masses and that the authoritarian leaders identified with those ideologies represented the *vox populi*. The reformist communists, in turn, still proclaim the essentially democratic character of original Leninism and do not deviate from the tenet that pure Leninists have always been the true exponents of the people's democratic goals, the standard bearers of "people's democracy."

This *reductio ad absurdum* of historic realities by all users - in fact, misusers - of the term "democracy" as reflective of the political culture and traditions of Eastern Europe needs to be clarified as we try to place the "Takeover" and its aftermath in the proper historic context of the twentieth century. And that will be attempted in the pages that follow.

Casting aside, for the moment, all definitions of democracy that deny individual rights, human and political, that reject the individual's rights to liberty and property and pluralistic participation in the determination of the political order, we may well ask to what extent was "bourgeois democracy" representative of the political culture and experience of the peoples of Eastern Europe at the end of World War II. We may also question the corollary claims of anti-fascist and anti-communist leaders that they were the true representatives of the peoples' interests at that time.

Caution must be exercised since, axiomatically, all leaders who sought recognition by the victorious Allies had to have been identified with the "struggle for liberation from fascism" and, preferably, with a long-standing commitment to "democracy."

It is fair to say that at least in a few countries of Eastern Europe, those in which urbanism and bourgeois capitalism had created conditions for meaningful participatory democracy, such as Czechoslovakia and, to a lesser extent and largely on regional bases, also Hungary, Romania, Poland and Yugoslavia, liberal, peasant, social democratic, and socialist parties had sought and, on occasion, commanded the political allegiance of significant segments of the population. It is also fair to say that most of these political organizations were generally uncooperative with totalitarian forces, fascist or communists, during the interwar and war years. To say, however, that they were representative of the interests of their constituencies and of their political culture, that they overtly opposed the authoritarian regimes of Hungary's Horthy, of the Poland of the colonels, of the royal dictatorships of Bulgaria, Romania, and Yugoslavia or, perhaps more significantly, first the "fascists" and later in the war, the communists, would be less than accurate.

It has been argued, of course, that the primary function of political organizations in the developing societies that had to adapt to the world that emerged from and after the dissolution of the European imperial order of the Habsburgs, Romanovs, Germans, and Ottoman Turks was the political education of the masses. Participatory democracy with guaranteed human, property, and political rights, as imposed by the Western Allies, was by-and-large a novel experience for the majority of the peoples of Eastern Europe, accustomed as they were to paternalistic, divinely-ordained and religiously-sanctioned socio-political orders. Moreover, since the dissolution of the empires was legitimized by the principle of national self-determination, which the Allies regarded as entirely compatible with the "democratic" aspirations of the inhabitants of the succession states, nationalism and democracy were deemed prerequisites for the successful entry of Eastern Europe in the community of a peace-loving and prosperous continent. Given the absurdity - based on either cynicism, ignorance, or both - of these assumptions advocated by Woodrow Wilson and his fellow peacemakers, the "historic" and the nascent political organizations committed, or paying lip-service, to democratic principles were faced with well-nigh impossible tasks and, more often than not, with losing battles.

We need not recapitulate the political history of the interwar years. Suffice it to say that, in general, nationalism proved to be incompatible with bourgeois democracy and that non- or anti-democratic forces were readily able to exploit that contradiction and other objective conditions that militated against successful democratization of the succession states. Unpopular view as it may be, the historic fact is that the largely illiterate peasant masses that comprised the great majority of the population of Eastern Europe at the end of World War I had virtually no acquaintance with democratic means of political expression or, for that matter, any meaningful interest in politics as such. The peasantry's primary concern was the securing of the land received through agrarian reforms or through redefinition of property rights in the new Eastern Europe of greater or smaller national states. Identification of the peasants' interest with political organizations, primarily peasant parties, was evident in most East European countries - most notably in Bulgaria - but whether that identification superseded the traditional allegiance to the paternalistic monarchy and church is questionable. The historic experience would tend to indicate that the effectiveness of peasant parties was limited whenever crown and church were in opposition to, or non-supportive of, their plans or programs. Moreover, the leadership of the peasant parties incorporated elements not necessarily recognized by the peasants as "one of their own" - urban intellectuals, nationalist businessmen and, in certain instances, even liberal Jews - which mitigated the ability of the parties to gain the unequivocal allegiance of the peasantry, to consolidate the gains secured by the peasantry at the end of the war and, above all, to prevent the "splitism" which weakened the peasantry's potential political power and strengthened that of non- or anti-democratic forces.

Inasmuch as traditional conservative elements sought to prevent "peasant democracy" and, as such, to at least limit the effectiveness of peasant organizations, the political dynamics of the interwar years focused, directly or indirectly, on controlling and directing the politicization of the process of adaptation of rural societies to the urbanization and industrialization of the succession states.

The modernization of East European societies to which all leaders had committed themselves, *volens nolens*, at the end of the war and corollary migration from village to town did entail rapid urban and industrial development. This dual process resulted, as is generally known, in disaffection primarily by the young who settled in urban centers either as workers, in generally primitive industrial or commercial establishments, or as students. The disaffection was enhanced in most East European countries by the multi-ethnic character of urban settlements and, particularly, by ownership of commercial and industrial enterprises by Jews, not to mention the disproportionate Jewish presence in educational institutions. The ensuing exacerbation of xenophobia and anti-Semitism - never alien in Eastern Europe - was exploited by nationalists, by influential conservative groups in the military and clerical establishments, and by the monarchies. The fact that Bolshevism was identified with Judaism, especially in Hungary, Poland, and Romania, and viewed as a threat to the interests of the inhabitants of the new nation states, the presumed "Judeo-Bolshevik" threat was used as an instrument for discrediting the peasant parties, generally labeled as leftist, as well as other political organizations - socialist, social-democratic and, of course, communist - which presumably were unable to combat the "enemy" with the required vigor.

The task of discrediting political organizations at least nominally concerned with problems related to the working class was much simpler than that of compromising the peasant parties. Most communist organizations were virtually dismantled, if not always legally dissolved, following the Béla Kun fiasco, the unsuccessful rebellions sponsored by Moscow in Bessarabia, the Soviet-Polish war, the assassination of Stamboliski, to mention but a few of the communist actions deemed threatening to the political and socio-economic interests of leaders and citizens alike. Socialist and social-democrats were generally self-styled bourgeois and intellectual spokesmen for the interests of a largely apolitical labor force which did not necessarily identify its own interests with those of its urban, white collar champions. Through invocation of the Judeo-communist threat and promises, more often than actual measures, designed at least to placate if not "buy off" the working class and the usually weak trade unions, the conservative political parties with the support of conservative ruling establishments and of military and religious leaders were, as a rule, able to contain strikes and labor demonstrations even during the years of the Great Depression. However, such actions by the "left" were almost invariably exploited for legitimizing consolidation of autocratic power by "defenders" of the nation and national interests. They were also exploited by the radical "right."

Thus, it may well be asked whether pluralistic -even if "controlled" or "guided" - democracy was ever regarded as a desirable formula for governance of the succession states by elites and masses alike. The evidence would speak against acceptance of the traditional answers which would blame the failure of democracy on the irresponsible attitudes and actions of overly partisan, radical organizations and leaders of the "left" and even more so of the "right" and their external sponsors or supporters - the Russian Bolsheviks and, respectively, the Italian Fascists and German Nazis.

The fact is that radical political organizations of the right or of the left were opposed to political pluralism. However, with few exceptions, for most of the interwar period the radical communist left had virtually no constituency and its political activities, within and outside the parliamentary framework, could not jeopardize the security of any succession state and, as such, justify the abandonment of the democratic experiment. Such influence as could be, and occasionally was, exerted by Moscow and the Comintern was largely negated by the heavily Jewish leadership that could be, and mostly was, readily discredited and persecuted in the name of national and nationalist interests. The radical right, which emerged as a force in East European politics in the late twenties and early 1930s, had greater power, but such power as it had was also subject to direction from the conservative ruling elites.

The radical right did enjoy significant support among the peasantry and working class, in part because many of its members - youths of peasant or proletarian origin - could identify with the masses. This was particularly true of such organizations as the Romanian Iron Guard or the Hungarian Arrow Cross whose populism and anti-urbanism were expressed primarily through virulent and violent anti-Semitism. Their actions and ideologies, such as they were, appealed also to much of the petty bourgeoisie and, at least in the early stages, to conservative political groups that preferred not to be expressly identified with overtly anti-democratic and anti-Semitic actions. Most notable in this respect was the support provided to the radical right by "clerico-fascists" and like opponents of political pluralism and "democratic experiments" in general. While it is true that power reverted to the radical right only after the massive intervention by Nazi Germany and Fascist Italy in the internal affairs of the countries of Eastern Europe, it is also true that conservative political forces, through skillful exploitation of the inroads made by the radical right, managed to gain either outright control of the political order of the succession states or at least to erode the initial commitment to pluralistic, democratic politics and witness the decline and eventual collapse of liberal or moderate governments in the thirties. And it should be noted that these processes of "de-democratization" were in full swing even before Mussolini or Hitler could be held responsible for the "collapse of democracy" in Eastern Europe.

It is undeniable that Fascist Italy and Nazi Germany were supportive of the radical right and also that rightist politicians were more often than not sympathetic toward the aims and policies of the Axis. It would be fallacious, however, to assume that the radical right and its organizations were creatures of Mussolini or Hitler. Rather, Iron Guardists, clerico-fascists, and similar groups expressed views compatible with nationalist ideologies held dear by most conservative politicians and by a significant proportion of the inhabitants of the succession states. For indeed, nationalism was the *lingua franca* of irredentists and anti-revisionists, of anti-Semites and anti-communists. That Hitler, Mussolini, and Stalin, each in his own way, exploited and encouraged irredentism for the attainment of his own revisionist and imperialist goals is unquestionable, but that exploitation was possible only because conditions for "divide and conquer" were ripe in the 1930s. Under the prevailing "objective conditions," the several moderate and democratically-inclined political parties that were in power throughout most of the interwar years in Czechoslovakia and occasionally, if briefly, in other countries of Eastern Europe could never establish a strong enough political base and develop a devoted enough constituency to resist the anti-democratic, separatist, extremist, anti-communist, and other negative forces that led, gradually, to the establishment of dictatorships or authoritarian regimes. The internal forces opposing democracy were generally acting if not with the formal consent of the population, at least without meaningful opposition. The fact that the anti-democratic forces succeeded in their goals does not, however, suggest that they were unequivocally supportive of Hitler's and Mussolini's. And that was so because the Axis was ready to undermine its supporters and sympathizers in the succession states whenever it suited the Führer's or Duce's interests. Yet, this apparent contradiction does not imply, as has so often been suggested, that democracy failed in interwar Eastern Europe because of external pressures which caused the adoption of, or support for, anti-democratic attitudes and measures by political organizations and by people at large which would not have occurred under different international circumstances. Rather, it failed or, more correctly, failed to take root, because the preconditions for pluralistic democracy were almost uniformly missing in the historic experience and political and cultural values, traditions, and mentalities of the majority of the peoples of the succession states and of the ruling elites.

The prevalent contemporary view is that the peoples of Eastern Europe, no matter what their attitudes toward the Nazi penetration, conquest, or domination of their countries, were generally united, toward the end of the war, in their massive opposition to totalitarianism and committed to the restoration of the democracy which generally eluded them in the interwar years. Moreover, a significant majority of the same people who had identified the Soviet Union as a "liberating" force from "fascism" that would allow them to achieve democratic goals, realized by 1944 that "liberation" to Stalin meant only the substitution of one dictatorship for another. Whether the majority of the population also realized that "people's democracy" had little, if anything, in common with Western democracy or, for that matter, that communist rule would be the least compatible with the historic traditions and political culture of Eastern Europe and, as such, the least desirable alternative to any form of governance experienced during the interwar and wartime years is, however, uncertain. What is certain is that the majority of political leaders and organizations that emerged toward the end of World War II were not committed to democracy so much as to anti-communism; in fact, their democratic tendencies and pronunciamentos generally represented a disclaimer of their presumably involuntary "cooperative" attitudes toward wartime regimes. There were, of course, exceptions - particularly among the so-called "governments in exile" - but, perhaps cynically, the democratic commitments of those governments assumed exaggerated proportions as the likelihood of their ever assuming power vanished after the nefarious agreements between the Western Allies and the Soviet Union. It should not be forgotten that "collaborationists" with the Axis were rather numerous even before the outbreak of the war in Hungary, Yugoslavia, Albania, Romania, and even Czechoslovakia and that their number increased markedly during the war itself. The *Ustasha*, Marshal Antonescu, Father Hlinka and others have been condemned for their wartime activities but surely they did not lack in actual or tacit support from other political leaders and, for that matter, even from a significant part of the population. Also of interest is the fact that the "resistance" forces, be they "democratic" or overtly "anti-fascist," were generally "fighting fascism" not in a western, democratic sense, but usually in defense of "nationalism" or in support of the "struggle for liberation" from fascism through the military and political efforts of the "democratic" Soviet Union. That the pro-Soviet, if not necessarily communist-sponsored and directed, "resistance" fighters were able to dupe the population when the defeat of Nazi Germany seemed inevitable after the collapse of Mussolini and Soviet victories in the post-Stalingrad period, is not surprising given the misleading legitimation of "anti-fascist" activities by men such as Tito or the Greek communists, the cynical manipulations of Stalin and, in their own ways, those of Roosevelt and Churchill. But lest we forget, few of the East European political leaders who could champion democracy by the end of the war had voiced more than token opposition to the ruling wartime regimes even in the waning stages of the conflict. Whether their failure to do so was prompted by the great risks involved in opposing totalitarian regimes acting under Nazi orders or in consort with Hitler's Germany, or whether it was based on the realization of the inevitability of Soviet domination of Eastern Europe and of the likely realities of such domination, is unclear. It would appear, however, as if the threat of communism and Soviet retaliation against all political groups other than those subservient to Stalin was deemed to be more fatal to their existence than acquiescence to non-communist totalitarian or authoritarian rule. The corollary question of whether "closet" democrats would have been more active in the late stages of the war had their secretive or indirect contacts with Britain and the United States met with encouragement as regards the dangers of communist liberation, is also difficult to answer. It is reasonable to assume, however, that the naive or cynical responses of the British and Americans dampened any realistic hopes for avoidance of the substitution of a communist for a "fascist" dictatorship at the end of the war. Because of the unwillingness of the United States and England to unmask the presumed "democratic" intentions of the Soviet Union, the potentially, and few actual, democratic political groups had to opt for cooperation with the communist-led "resistance" and "liberating" forces in the forlorn hope that the United States, at least, would prevent outright Soviet takeovers and resultant Stalinist dictatorships in postwar Eastern Europe. There was, indeed, Hobson's choice: was it more important to discredit the compromised regimes and participate in pseudo-democratization in the hope of communist moderation or was it best to abstain from any participation in communist-infiltrated or dominated political coalitions while promoting democratic ideals? As it is known, few indeed were those political leaders who chose the latter alternative but, in truth, even the number who chose the former was quite limited.

The question may rightly be asked, then, whether abstinence or opportunism were the most realistic approaches given the "objective conditions" prevailing at the end of World War II? If a communist takeover was inevitable, as the vast majority of political leaders and politically-conscious population surmised, the only hope was reliance on Western actions designed to moderate Stalin's aims and methods. To actively counter the communists was an option for the foolhardy, or politicians in exile, since the communist-dominated organizations championing "people's democracy" as a reward for victory over "fascism" were sufficiently persuasive, at least initially, to appeal to the politically naive or indifferent masses as the fact that the "glorious Soviet armies" were reinforcing the "democratic, anti-fascist" forces in a manner that cast doubts about the trustworthiness of the propaganda did not, per se, exclude for the gullible the possibility of moderation in the "Takeover." It was only after the "democratic fronts" became more and more exposed as instruments of Soviet policy and of Stalin's true goals, as the leadership of these organizations became more and more infiltrated by alien elements, mostly Jews and foreigners, as the role of the "liberating" Soviet armed forces and Soviet political advisers and representatives became all the more evident, that reality began to awaken and impress the masses. Nevertheless, even then political leaders of the "historic parties," who in one way or another cooperated in or tolerated the "democratization" of Eastern Europe orchestrated and conducted by the Soviet Union, were willing to seek further compromises as long as the communists limited their definition of "fascists" and sought, at least pro forma, cooperation with those who could be identified with the traditional interests of the people. The convergence of the communist claims of representing the "workers and working peasantry" with those of other presumed representatives of the workers' and peasants' interests - the socialists and agrarians, respectively - still deluded those segments of the population that were traditionally anti-urban and anti-bourgeois capitalist and, as such, accepted collaboration of socialist and agrarian leaders with communists as a feasible, if not necessarily normal, relationship. The fact is that "democracy," in the western pluralistic and participatory sense, was not much of an issue for the majority of the peoples of Eastern Europe as soon as that political alternative became utopian after the end of the war. However, the true nature of "people's democracy" was realistically faced only by a small number of politically-conscious individuals who, unlike the majority of their compatriots, understood the significance of "salami tactics" and the total cynicism and indifference of the Western Allies to the gradual and inevitable conquest of Eastern Europe by Stalin and fellow communists. Individual details may have differed in terms of specific geopolitical and internal conditions but, in fact, the differences between Tito's tactics and success and those of Dimitrov, Ana Pauker, Rákosi, and even Gotttwald were in essence the same. Without the support of the Western Allies - in fact, with their acquiescence of gradual communist takeovers - the few democratic forces present in wartime and early postwar Eastern Europe could under no circumstances secure a lasting foothold in the Stalinist regimes imposed or supported by the Soviet Union.

Yet, in our opinion, the takeovers should not necessarily be viewed as a confrontation between "democracy" and "totalitarianism," as a communist destruction of actual or potential democratic forces. To assume that the defeat of "fascism" was due to the opposition of the peoples of Eastern Europe to totalitarianism which resulted, after years of experience under the "fascist heel" in an awareness of the merits of democracy, if not necessarily in a revival of alleged democratic sentiments and practices stifled by totalitarianism, is an exaggeration at best and a cynical propaganda ploy at worst. The native "fascist" dictatorships were generally accepted, albeit more with resignation than enthusiasm, throughout most of Eastern Europe. The defeat of the Axis was welcomed as it meant the end of a cruel war. "Liberation from Fascism" would have aroused enthusiasm had it been carried out by the democratic forces of the Western Allies; however, it aroused suspicions, and often fears, as the democratic liberating forces were those of the Soviet Union. But even those liberators would have been acceptable, or at least tolerable, had the communist-dominated "democratic" leaders been selective in implementation of their plans by insuring their compatibility with prevailing political cultures and traditions. However, the gradual desecration of religion and religious institutions, the attack on private property rights, the elevation to power of Jews and "Moscovites" unidentified with national cultures and traditions failed to compensate for the "reforms" that eliminated the political power of the bourgeoisie and urban and rural "capitalists." And, ultimately, the presence of "liberating" Soviet armed forces, combined with the ruthless exploitation of the "Soviet Bloc" by the Soviet Union and its satraps, led to the resurgence of two fundamental and deepening elements of the political culture of Eastern Europe - anti-communism and nationalism.

Anti-communism was an option available only to Eastern European political leaders in exile and to the ethnic diasporas. Anti-communism was not, however, necessarily equated or identified with democratic revulsion against totalitarianism. In fact, except when such identification was required by the political environment of the host country or stemmed from genuine conviction that democracy was the answer to the problems of postwar Eastern Europe, anti-communist activities were directed and orchestrated by conservative, authoritarian, and quite frequently "neo-fascist" politicians. Nationalism, however, was adopted by nearly all anti-communists who held the "Bolsheviks" responsible for the desecration of national historic and cultural traditions, for conquering by force and illegitimate means the national states of Eastern Europe and establishing the "evil empire." The political goal of the governments, national committees, and other political organizations in exile and of most of the politically conscious and concerned members of the diaspoara became defined as a "crusade for freedom" from communism for the satellites of the Soviet Union. The essential incompatibility between historic nationalism and communism and Western bourgeois democracy was often deliberately ignored by the sponsors of "liberating" movements - mostly the United States - who, shortly after the total communist takeover of Eastern Europe, equated the crusade for freedom with liberation of "captive nations" yearning for western democracy. That incompatibility, however, was known to, and capitalized upon by, non-democratic leaders of liberation movements, mostly in Western Europe. Aware as they were of the general absence of democratic traditions and of the paternalistic, authoritarian, and conservative political culture common to Eastern Europe, they rightly claimed that anti-communism does not imply democratic sentiments and goals but rather replacement of the heathen, Judeo-communist dictatorships by conservative, authoritarian, nationalist regimes.

The new rulers of Eastern Europe including, of course, Stalin himself, also realized from an early date that limited identification of communism with nationalism was politically expedient not only to counter external propaganda but also, and primarily, to allow them to assume the role of executors of the peoples' historic interests and of the national historic traditions. The obvious falsifications of the aim of the people, defined as the struggle for the attainment of socialism, did not erase the anti-communism of the inhabitants of the Soviet Bloc. Nor did, for that matter, the redefinition of historic nationalism as "socialist patriotism" correspond to the historic truth. However, the co-opting of nationalism and the enunciation of the doctrine of "national roads to socialism" relieved, at least partially, the anti-Soviet sentiments of the East Europeans.

The efficacy of making nationalism an essential element of the political dialogue and platforms of all parties concerned with Eastern Europe is questionable; what is important, however, is that the common denominator - nationalism - was considered an integral and indispensable part of the political culture and historic traditions of Eastern Europe. Gradually, too, all parties made "democracy" an integral part of the political dialogue and platforms, albeit in incompatible definitions and utilizations of the term. The communists never deviated from the premise that they were the trustees and fulfillers of the peoples' "democratic" goals as evidenced, inter alia, in the retention of the term "people's democracy" for identification of the nature and status of such countries as Hungary, Poland, and Bulgaria. Other Eastern European countries, such as Romania and Czechoslovakia, which deleted "people's democracy" in favor of "socialist republic" merely regarded "socialist" as a more perfect "democracy" on the assumption that communism itself was the ultimate expression of the peoples' historic "democratic" goals. It is worth noting that even in 1989, reformist communists did not necessarily reject that definition of "democracy"; they merely admitted to errors in the formulation and implementation of policies by dogmatic interpreters of Marxism-Leninism.

It is, however, more important to note that even after the "revolutions" of 1989, the establishment of western bourgeois democracy has been neither a *sine qua non* nor a realistic goal for the majority of the inhabitants of Hungary, Poland, and other countries of Eastern Europe. Few indeed are those in Eastern Europe, or for that matter even in the west, who believe in the likelihood of genuine democratization, at least in the near future. The chances of developing meaningful political organizations that could participate in determining a democratic course for one or another country appears to be limited. The destruction of the moderate liberal urban bourgeoisie and of the petty rural bourgeoisie, and of the political parties identified with or representative of their interests, would require a lengthy restructuring of the socio-economic and political orders. Besides, the world economic conditions, as different as they are now from what they were before World War II, would virtually - at least in the near term - preclude the establishment of viable "bourgeois capitalist" and corollary "bourgeois democratic" systems. Economic and social changes do not require, in the view of the majority of East Europeans, coincidence of political orders; of greater importance is the restoration of human and property rights. Those rights need not be those granted by the American constitution or, for that matter, by the first and fifth amendments to that unique document; they do, however, encompass the right to free practice of religion, the right to private property and unhindered disposition thereof, the right to free association and expression. Political paternalism by a benevolent bureaucratic state would be acceptable as long as the abusive elements which characterized the monolithic communist police states of Eastern Europe would not recur.

This perception is incorporated in the political platforms of non- or pseudo-democratic opponents of communism who advocate the restoration of property and religious rights, however not in conformity with formulae devised by western bourgeois democrats and their East European adherents and counterparts, but with what they consider to be the historic legacy of pre-communist Eastern Europe - "Orthodoxy, Autocracy, Nationality." The neo-Slavophiles or, rather, the "neo-Fascists," are persuaded that the political culture of the majority of the peoples of Eastern Europe is rooted in religion, paternalism, and the quest for independence within a national state ruled by the ethnic majority for the benefit of that majority and that those who are not "one of us" from a religious, national, and cultural standpoint could only hope for toleration. In other words, the alternative to "national socialism" of the communist variety is not western socialism or democracy, but "national socialism" of a "populist democratic" variety. The fact that these views appear to be popular with a large number of anti-communist émigrés, with much of the diaspora, and apparently also with significant segments of the peoples of Eastern Europe itself, one may well wonder whether conventional interpretations of the significance of the "Takeover" in the history of Eastern Europe are not questionable at best.

To summarize our views: the "Takeover" was inevitable and successful not because it was compatible with the desiderata of the peoples and political leaders of Eastern Europe but because of the lack of alternatives available at the end of World War II. The internal democratic forces were weak not only because they were de facto obliterated during the war but also because, with few exceptions, they never had broadly-based constituencies or, for that matter, extensive support from the people. The rejection of "fascism" was not necessarily the result of an explosion of democratic sentiments by the East Europeans which had to be hidden during the war; it was, in many cases, a necessity to avoid a greater evil - heathen Bolshevism - and to secure the support of the Western Allies in the face of the Soviet threat. The actions of the Allies which facilitated the "Takeover," with cynical disregard of the consequences of that expansion of Soviet power, rendered any democratic resolution of the fate of postwar Eastern Europe impossible. The Russians were *"bon pour l'Orient"* and *"l'Orient"* was good for the Russians. While the Western attitude was characteristic and hardly based on cognizance of factors other than strategic and geopolitical, the fact is that the political culture and historic experience of most of Eastern Europe was not incompatible with that of pre-communist Russia. Russian intervention in "wars of national independence" and in World War I, for instance, and resultant occupations of parts of Eastern Europe were often viewed as advantageous and congruent with national interests; in fact, more often than not, Russia was the "Big Brother." This is to say that had Stalin kept the promises made to his wartime allies and had he been true to his own propaganda, "liberation" and the ensuing takeover would not have been regarded as a disaster either by the West or by the East Europeans themselves. But Stalin's totalitarianism differed greatly from the traditional authoritarian, paternalistic, nationalist political patterns prevalent in Eastern Europe, and his "orthodoxy, autocracy, nationality" was incompatible with that of the "liberated" countries. The takeover destroyed the traditional conservative forces - church, aristocracy, bourgeoisie, and peasantry - by means far more brutal than any known in modern times. His, and his satraps' in Eastern Europe, was the wrong orthodoxy, autocracy, and nationality and, despite cosmetic efforts at seeking identification of the communist order and state with the pre-communist and historic political cultural traditions, communism of the Stalinist variety remained unacceptable. The collapse of communism then does not necessarily entail acceptance of bourgeois democracy as an ideology and system representative of, or even compatible with, the political cultural traditions of the "developing" East European national, and nationalist, states of the twentieth century. There are other alternatives.

CHAPTER SEVEN

THE REVIVAL OF THE POLITICAL RIGHT IN POST-COMMUNIST EASTERN EUROPE: THE HISTORICAL PERSPECTIVE

1989 has been hailed as the year when the decades-long struggle of the peoples of Eastern Europe against communist tyranny, for democracy, was won. Inasmuch as 1945 was likewise hailed as the year when the same peoples' struggle against fascist tyranny, for democracy, was won, it seems reasonable to question the optimism of those who hailed the death of totalitarianism and the yearning for democracy of the peoples of Eastern Europe.

The revival of the political Right in post-communist Eastern Europe is explicable in more ways than one; yet, all explanations are rooted in the historic realities and experiences of the twentieth century. It would indeed be a grave error to assume - as has been assumed by naive or cynical intellectuals and politicians - that fascism and communism were aberrations incompatible with the democratic convictions and aspirations of the peoples of Eastern Europe and that the so-called struggles against authoritarian and/or totalitarian regimes were demonstrations of implacable opposition to non-democratic orders. The well known slogans, applicable on a wider geopolitical scale than the East European, that "Fascism is dead" and "Communism is dead" have proven to be premature obituaries written by ignorant or self-serving political leaders who, quite frequently, have shouted "Long live Democracy" by necessity rather than by choice.

It is fair to say that the moving force and common denominator of the "peoples' historic struggle for liberation" - equated with national independence and statehood - has been nationalism. It is also fair to say that, with minor exceptions, East European nationalism was by definition anti-imperialist, rooted in the spirit of avenging the humiliations inflicted upon their nations by foreign oppressors, characterized by intolerance of ethnic and religious diversity and, as such, not committed to the spirit of Wilsonian democracy. Nor were the adoption of market economies, party pluralism, constitutionalism, and guarantees of human and/or minority rights prerequisites for the functioning of the independent states established at the end of World War I. Rather, it was the safeguarding of territorial gains or the recouping of territorial losses resulting from the collapse of the Central and East European historic empires that were the primary concern of the political leaders of interwar Eastern Europe. It is not that the peoples of interwar Eastern Europe, and many of their leaders, were necessarily adverse to democracy but it is true that democratic forms and practices had to be subordinated to national interests and that such interests were defined as a function of historic nationalism.

The imposition of democratic constitutions by the victorious powers, on the one hand, and the threat of communism from Bolshevik Russia, on the other, were regarded as incompatible, if not inimical, to historic nationalism. The socio-economic and political readjustments implicit in democratic constitutionalism, which sought solutions by political compromise involving organizations representative of all classes in society and of all ethnic and religious groups, was almost as unacceptable to most nationalists as the threat of "Bolshevization." Indeed, the various socio-economic reforms in agriculture and industry and the unconditional granting of full political and civil rights to ethnic and religious minorities which the successor states undertook, mostly reluctantly under international pressures, solidified the opposition to democratization whether of the Wilsonian or Leninist varieties. It is that very political opposition, comprising initially the conservative nationalist elites and their political organizations, that has been characterized as the "political Right" in interwar Eastern Europe.

Although differences in the specific issues addressed and their constituencies varied from country to country during those years, the "political Right," whether in its extremist, radical, authoritarian, quasi-Fascist form or in the more conventional "Christian-Democratic" one, displayed common characteristics. Albeit with differences in degree of emphasis, the "political Right" was chauvinistic, xenophobic, anti-Semitic, anti-communist, supportive of and supported by the religious and military establishments.

Inasmuch as the characteristics attributed to the Right were not generally absent even in centrist or, for that matter to a certain degree even in left-of-center political organizations, not to mention in the several "Royal dictatorships" and authoritarian regimes, it seems essential to note that the "political Right" was the dominant force in East European politics before World War II and that its premises and programs were generally, if not necessarily, endorsed, or at least not opposed, by the majority of the peoples of Eastern Europe. That was certainly the case in Hungary and Romania and perhaps only to a lesser degree in Croatia and Slovakia. It was true in post-Stamboliiski Bulgaria, post-Pilsudski Poland, post-Fan Noli Albania and, at least in the 1930s, in Slovenia.

The contention advanced by apologists of the Right that the turn away from evolving democracy was caused by the threat of Bolshevism and by the destabilization of the interwar East European political systems by Fascist Italy and Nazi Germany is generally baseless. The threat of Bolshevism was indeed true in Hungary, Romania, and Poland. It did indeed contribute to the consolidation of the power of Admiral Horthy in the post-Bela Kun period and to the rise in the level of anti-Semitism in Hungary. However, Hungarian irredentism and socio-economic conservatism, both key factors in the success of the moderate Right, antedated and survived the Hungarian Soviet Republic. Nor can it be said that the radical, crudely anti-Semitic Arrow Cross was the creature of the Bolshevik threat or of Hitler or Mussolini. Similarly in Romania, Bolshevik Russia's irredentism with respect to Bessarabia was much less of a factor in the evolution of the moderate and radical Right than opposition by the moderate Right to the agrarian reforms and the increase in the number of "leftist" political parties which threatened the monopoly of power of the Bucharest establishment and of the radical Right to the influx of Jews from Bessarabia and Bukovina into northeastern Romania. The radically anti-communist and anti-Semitic League of National Christian Defense and the clearly fascist League of the Archangel Michael - the Iron Guard - were home grown, antedated the Nazis, acted independently of any support from Hitler or Mussolini before the mid-1930s and only with minimal support from Nazi Germany in the late 1930s.

The Bolshevik threat, such as it was, ended - at least temporarily - after the victorious Polish-Soviet War of 1919-20. However, continuing fear of communism, though less than the destruction of the parliamentary system by Pilsudski and the rise in anti-Semitism because of social disloca- tion and economic factors, enabled the Right to take control of the Polish political system in the mid-1930s. It is noteworthy that neither the moderate Right, headed by Roman Dmowski's National Party, nor radical Right parties such as the National Radical Camp or the Falanga were creatures of Nazi Germany; in fact, they were as anti-German as anti- Russian. On the other hand, the significance of the close association with the Roman Catholic Church of both the moderate and radical Right, based as it was on shared anti-communism and anti-Semitism, should not be overlooked.

To an even greater extent than in Poland, the role of the Catholic Church as supporter of the political Right was crucial in the interwar years in Croatia, Slovenia, and Slovakia, none of which were threatened by Bolshevism or imperiled by the rise of Fascism and Nazism. The Catholic Church in these lands, and for that matter elsewhere in Eastern Europe, was by definition anti-communist and, more often than not, also anti-Semitic, anti-Orthodox, anti-Protestant, and anti-Moslem. It was also invariably conservative and influential in politics. In Croatia, it was most supportive of the nationalist opponents of Greater Serbia, the so-called "Right wing" of the Croatian Peasant Party, but at least part of the hierarchy embraced the "Clerical fascist" principles which guided the less moderate Frank Party and, for that matter, even the extremist *Ustasha*. And that support, as well as the political organizations themselves, with the exception of the *Ustasha*, antedate and/or were unrelated to either the threat of Bolshevism or the rise of German or Italian totalitarianism.

Opposition to Serbian domination of Yugoslavia's political life was led, in Slovenia, by the Slovene Clerical Party, headed by the Catholic Monsignor Anton Korosek, while in Slovakia, political opposition to Czech domination of Czechoslovakia's political and economic life, as well as to Hungarian revisionism, was the *raison d'être* of the Slovak People's Party, headed by Father Andrew Hlinka. Again, neither the moderate Right Slovene Clerical Party nor the extreme Right Slovak People's Party were creatures of anti-Bolshevism or of Nazism or Italian Fascism. Their roots were native and reflective of conditions internal to Yugoslavia and Czechoslovakia; their "Clerical-fascism" was a genuine political phenomenon comparable with the Clerical Fascist movements of Austria, Spain, and Portugal.

Fear of Bolshevism and direct influence of Italian Fascism did, however, play a role in the evolution of the Right in Bulgaria and Albania. The "peasant democracy" established under Stamboliiski and the presence of an active Bulgarian Communist Party, subservient to Moscow, was feared by the conservative bureaucratic and military forces, as well as by the monarchy, and hated by the extreme Right, ultra-nationalist Internal Macedonian Revolutionary Organization (IMRO) which was supported overtly by Mussolini. The military and royal dictatorships that took charge of Bulgarian political life in the mid-1920s were clearly anti-communist and mostly pro-Italian, even though they sought to destroy the power of the terrorist IMRO. However, the Bulgarian Right, whether extremist or moderate, did not rely on the support of the Orthodox Church and revealed no anti-Semitic tendencies. Similarly, the Albanian Right, led by Ahmet Zogu (later King Zog I) justified its authoritarian, nationalist regime because of its victory over the "progressive" Monsignor Fan Noli, whose governmental reforms antagonized the landed beys. The Right maintained itself in power, with support from Fascist Italy, between 1924 and 1939.

It would be incorrect to overemphasize the power of the Right or to dismiss the relevance of democratic, usually centrist, political parties in interwar Eastern Europe. It would also be incorrect to attribute the success of the Right primarily to its anti-Bolshevism, anti-Semitism, xenophobia, and intolerance toward ethnic, national, or religious minorities. It is true, for instance, that socio-economic factors related to urbanization, the Great Depression, and to unemployment were influential, if not decisive, in the rise of the Right, especially in Romania, Hungary, and Poland. Yet, it is also incorrect to suggest that the Right, especially in its extremist forms, was an aberration and that its political power would eventually have been reduced, if not totally obliterated, had the democratic forces been given more time to develop their programs, both domestic and foreign. It is true that external factors, related to the power of Nazi Germany and the consolidation of Stalin's power in the Soviet Union, enhanced the legitimacy and power of the Right on the eve of World War II and during the war. But it is also true that, as the generally-viewed "ultimate" exponent of nationalism, the Right had a solid base of support on the eve of the war as well as during the war. And that base did not disappear, albeit for a variety of reasons, even after the war.

It would be difficult to discern any meaningful opposition to the Nazi domination of Eastern Europe during World War II by the leadership or adherents of the centrist or leftist, officially or formally disbanded, political organizations. It would, however, be easy to discern collaboration of rightist organizations with the authoritarian regimes in power and, more significantly, the over support of Nazi Germany and/or Fascist Italy by the radical Right in Romania, Hungary, Croatia, and Slovakia. Whereas in Romania Marshal Antonescu and the Iron Guardists loyal to him justified their joining Hitler in the name of recovering territories illegally annexed by the Soviet Union in 1940, the very legitimacy of the Antonescu regime was derived from Orthodox Romanianism which, specifically, sought the exclusion of Jews from the Romanian body social and political, if not their physical extermination. No such rationale was evident in Hungary where the Horthy regime justified its pro-Axis stand by common opposition to communism and the USSR and where the Arrow Cross, in keeping with its extremist anti-Semitic and anti-communist policies, supported the Nazi goal of exterminating "Judeo-Communism" by military means and, in the case of the Jews, by means of the Holocaust. Father Hlinka and his more extremist collaborators were loyal to the Nazis but refrained from the physical extermination of the Jews. In Croatia, however, the *Ustasha* led by Ante Pavelich, while displaying no toleration toward Jews, focused their attention on the extermination of Serbs. What is more important, however, in terms of assessing the strength of the Right, is the attitude of the masses of Eastern Europe toward occupiers and native leaders during World War II. It seems fair to say that there was genuine support for Antonescu and Pavelich and general acceptance of the Hungarian and Slovak regimes, at least until the collapse of Nazi Germany seemed inevitable.

In view of subsequent developments it seems essential to consider the position of the East European Right outside Eastern Europe proper, either in the so-called "governments in exile" or as part of those members of diplomatic, economic, and cultural missions who chose to stay in belligerent or non-belligerent countries during the war years.

The governments in exile, specifically the Polish and Czech, included members of the moderate Right. Whereas the attitude of members of these governments toward the Soviet Union varied, all were united in anti-communism and anti-Nazism. What is less certain is the extent to which their *raison d'être* - liberation of their countries from fascism and/or communism - entailed the establishment, upon liberation, of truly democratic regimes. More is known about rifts in the ranks of anti-communist diplomats and intellectuals abroad where the anti-communism and anti-Nazism of the majority was based more on violations of their countries' national rights than of human, ethnic, minority, or religious rights. In fact, nationalism was the legitimizer of their opposition to Hitler and Stalin.

Generally forgotten in the euphoria generated first by the foreseeable, and later achieved, victory over the Nazis was the belief that all East European leaders outside Eastern Europe were anti-totalitarian and, as such, at least receptive to democracy. This, in fact, was hardly the case as a large number of such leaders and lesser followers were either in Germany or Austria during the war and an even larger number had relocated in Franco's Spain, Peron's Argentina, and other Central and Latin American countries. As western suspicions of the intentions of the Soviet Union increased the true colors of such individuals became discernible. Assuming the posture of champions of democracy or, at least, of liberal nationalists and, chiefly in Spain and Argentina, even of anti-communists and nationalists of the Right, the prewar East European Right reemerged as a potential political force by 1945 when Stalin's plans for a communist takeover of Eastern Europe became evident. In that respect the "non-resident" Right assumed the responsibilities of the "resident" Right which shared the common goal of anti-communism and restoration of national independence within the borders of pre-Munich Europe or, in the case of irredentists, of pre-World War I Europe.

Full coordination of external and internal rightist ideologies and programs became possible after 1989; however, interaction became evident, as well as important, as national communism evolved in post-Stalinist Eastern Europe. Initially, as the Kremlin's plan for the communist takeover evolved and eventually succeeded in the late 1940s, as well as during the early years of consolidation of communist power in the so-called "satellites," the political emigration denounced communism and the communist systems as alien to the national historic tradition. However, there were significant differences in the definition of that tradition, ranging from national independence within the confines of a democratic internal and international order to national independence within an authoritarian, nationalist, ethnocentric system similar to that envisaged, or achieved, by the traditional Right, or even the radical Right, during the interwar years. Whereas the leaders who advocated the restoration of democracy following what they hoped would be the proximate liberation from communism were, in the early years of the Cold War, in the majority, it is evident that the activist, extremist Right, located primarily in Spain, Latin America, and West Germany paid only compulsory lip service to democracy while reviving the shopworn thesis of the radical Right that their countries were victims of the Judeo-Communist conspiracy which the Christian Right had fought since the end of World War I.

It is fair to say that during the period of gradual communist takeover and early years of actual communist rule the views of the extreme Right were shared by much of the population of Eastern Europe. The Soviet Union was hardly the presumed "liberator from fascism" and the communists were anything but exponents of the democracy which the Western allies, and especially the United States, were expected to secure for postwar Eastern Europe. The growing resentment toward the East European communists and their patrons in the Kremlin was enhanced by the fact that much of the leadership, at both the Party and state levels, was Jewish. Whereas neither anti-communism nor anti-Russianism were tolerated by the new rulers, anti-Semitism was not officially condemned and, by the early 1950s, the purging of Jews in both leading and subordinate cadres occurred, if not on Stalin's orders, at least with his consent. As this was followed, after Stalin's death, by the gradual formulation of such doctrines as "socialist patriotism" and "national roads to socialism" which, in essence, reflected the communists' claim of being the executors of national historic legacies, nationalism officially resurfaced in communist Eastern Europe.

Inasmuch as the United States and its European allies showed little inclination to liberate Eastern Europe from communism, as most clearly revealed in 1956, the political emigration which sought restoration of national independence in democratic societies began to lose ground to the political Right. In fact, as "crusades for freedom" and "captive nations' weeks" fell by the wayside in the age of "peaceful coexistence" and the number of East Europeans allowed to emigrate to the West increased, the Right gained the upper hand. Much of the new emigration was militantly anti-communist but not necessarily pro-democracy. Rather, it joined co-nationals in the diaspora whose anti-communism and/or nationalism did not necessarily envisage democratization as a perquisite of post-communist political orders. In fact, more often than not, the recent immigrants reinforced the anti-communism of the diaspora and validated the Right's interpretation of national traditions which had to be preserved with a view to invalidating the communists' claims to national historic legacies.

While the moderate Right, generally supported by such organizations as Radio Free Europe, found no incompatibility between nationalism and democracy in a liberated Eastern Europe, the radical Right pretended to equate anti-communism with democracy while, in fact, it furthered neo-fascist positions. Their anti-communist tirades were based on denunciations of the communists as instruments of the Judeo-Bolshevik anti-national conspiracy as well as of Russian imperialism and as mortal enemies of the national Christian traditions of Eastern Europe. In turn, the East European communists, particularly in Romania and Poland, adopted increasingly more nationalistic stands emphasizing historic international animosities and conflicts, as well as anti-Semitism. Concurrently, the Catholic and Orthodox churches became more involved in politics, at least to the extent of encouraging, if not supporting, those aspects and elements of communist nationalism that were compatible with historic national traditions as expounded by the historic moderate and less-than-moderate political Right. For instance, in the 1980s anti-Turkish, pro-Macedonian, and corollary anti-Yugoslav policies became *de rigueur* in Bulgaria; the Transylvanian question in both internal and external aspects was back on the front burner in Romania and, though somewhat more moderately, also in Hungary; Croat-Serbian relations took a turn for the worse while Slovak nationalism, in both its anti-Czech and anti-Semitic garb, reared its head. Thus, the convergence of the traditional nationalism of the Right and the new one of the Left became increasing more evident on the eve of the collapse of the communist regimes in 1989.

While it is fair to say that the legitimacy and/or validity of communist nationalism was questioned by both the moderate and the extreme Right and also that the blueprint for political and social change in post-communist Eastern Europe differed in the case of the moderate and extremist anti-communist nationalists of the Right, it is evident that historic nationalism was the indispensable legitimizer of any political program that would replace the communists in "liberated" Eastern Europe. And it is also fair to say that in the competition for power among exponents of nationalism, the political Right had a distinct advantage over other political organizations after 1989.

The expectations, or hopes, of idealists that the collapse of communism would lead to the rapid democratization of the East European states proved illusory. And there were good reasons for that. Anti-communism did not necessarily envisage democracy as an alternative in Eastern Europe itself or in the East European political emigration abroad. The denial of allegiance to communism and the professing of a commitment to democracy by members of the apparatus and bureaucratic establishment was not less of a subterfuge for insuring political survival than the equating of anti-communism with a commitment to democracy used by seekers of political power from both inside and outside Eastern Europe. Both were devices used primarily because the "restoration of democracy" became a prerequisite for securing economic aid from the United States and Western Europe. This is not to say that the elimination of the onerous restrictions on freedom of speech, of the press and, above all, of religion was resisted by the first post-communist regimes or that these essential elements of democracy were not desired by the majority of the peoples of Eastern Europe. It is also true that party pluralism was reinstated together with freely-elected parliaments. But these freedoms were often used for non-democratic purposes, primarily by communist or opportunist converts to "democracy," as well as by neo-fascists who were gradually to shed their democratic garb.

Inasmuch as the "restoration of democracy" implied the existence of democracy, or at least of democratic parties, prior to the advent of communist totalitarianism, the western democracies lent their support to "historic parties" whose pre-1948 leaders had either been active abroad or survived the communist era at home, as well as to East European politicians who could persuade the West of their democratic proclivities. The litmus test was anti-communism, a firm commitment to a market economy, respect for minority and religious rights, for constitutionalism, and for all other normal prerequisites for democratic societies. As it turned out, and not surprisingly, the very notion of "restoration" was in fact baseless since it was founded on wrong assumptions and historic realities.

The leaders of the "historic parties" who returned to Eastern Europe were soon to realize that they were alienated from the population both because of their prolonged absence from their native countries and because of the obsolescence of their ideas. And that was also true, albeit to a lesser degree, for members of historic parties who sought to revive the ideas and programs of the 1920s and 1930s. Other political organizations, with names similar to those of the historic parties, or committed to the democratic principles advocated by the West, fared better only in countries such as Czechoslovakia, Hungary, and Poland largely because of direct western economic support presumably secured because of their commitment to development of market economies. However, what may prove decisive for the political evolution of post-communist Eastern Europe was the insistence of the West and of the favored Czech, Hungarian, and Polish "democratic" regimes on the rapid introduction of market economies as a prerequisite for economic assistance as well as, in selected cases, in making such economic assistance contingent upon the granting and guaranteeing of unlimited rights to national, ethnic, and religious minorities.

It may well be asked whether the linking of the requirement of the introduction of market economies with that of respect for human and minority rights was reflective of a commitment to democracy or of stratagems based on the political interests of the United States, Germany, Great Britain, and France. The equating of anti-communism with democracy, of market economies with democracy, of respect of minority and human rights with democracy, was at best unrealistic. The fact that these precepts were applied selectively tends to question the commitment of the western nations to the establishment of viable democratic states throughout the former Soviet empire.

Democracy in Eastern Europe was not to be reinstated, not even to be born again; it was to be introduced gradually in societies exposed for generations to relentless nationalism under authoritarian and/or totalitarian regimes, whether "fascist" or "communist." But that would have entailed recognition of the historic reality that "democracy" and democratic political organizations were a rare commodity in Eastern Europe both before and after World War I, that nationalism was the legitimizer of the East European states and political organizations of the interwar, wartime, and even communist periods, and that nationalism was by definition, if not intolerant of ethnic, national, or religious diversity, at best only marginally tolerant. What is less certain is whether massive economic assistance, in the form of a Marshall Plan for Eastern Europe, would have lessened the pains of transition from communism and/or totalitarianism to an eventual democracy. However, in the absence of such economic assistance and in the presence of massive poverty and rising economic expectations of the disaffected majority of East Europeans - including and, perhaps, especially the disenchanted youth - the insistence on the introduction of market economies, with corollary massive inflation and unemployment, was to lead to distrust of free economies and their advocates, to renewed support for the defunct regulated economic systems which at least guaranteed job security and a minimum subsistence level, to xenophobia, and particularly to anti-Semitism through the traditional association of Jews with economic matters, and to considerable support for the historic positions of the Right, both moderate and immoderate.

The radical Right in post-communist Romania bears a striking resemblance to that of the interwar period; the Right in Hungary has not abandoned its chauvinistic and anti-Semitic stance of earlier years anymore than has the Polish Right; the Slovak secessionists, although presumably leftist, are the heirs of the Slovak nationalist Right; the Croat nationalists have the support of the old and new *Ustasha*. What is more alarming for the future of democracy is the renewed acceptance by the vast majority of political parties of the need of identification of their plans and programs with the execution of the national historic legacy; in other words, that nationalism is the *sine qua non* for political success. As the exponents of East European nationalism have seldom made market economies and toleration of ethnic, national, and religious diversity a prerequisite for the achievement of the national historic legacy, it is quite likely in the event of further deterioration of the economic and political crises of Eastern Europe that the Right, old and new, moderate or extreme, will at least consolidate its present gains, if not necessarily become the dominant force in East European politics. And that would be all the more likely because of the convergence of the interests of the supporters of nationalist, anti-democratic, causes of the former Left and the traditional and new Right.

CHAPTER EIGHT

ROMANIA'S ROAD TO DEMOCRACY:
A QUESTIONABLE PAST, AN UNCERTAIN FUTURE

In the immediate aftermath of the collapse of the oppressive communist dictatorship of Nicolae Ceausescu in 1989, the euphoria of the "liberated" and "liberators," so manifest at the time, was perceived by optimists and the politically-ignorant at home and abroad as the restoration of the old and/or beginning of a new democratic era in Romania. Yet, within less than a month after the crucial events of late December, it became apparent that the "road to democracy" was blocked by opponents representative of the Romanian political tradition and that it was not about to be opened by outside experts in the "construction of democracy."

It was, indeed, easy enough to hail the collapse of communism in Romania by the ultimate victors in the Cold War in Washington, and by their less influential European acolytes, and to conclude that the Romanian anti-communist revolution was an expression of the people's undaunted quest for western democracy than to take into account the realities of the Romanians' historic experience. It was just as easy, but also more accurate, for the Romanian political emigration to regard the events of December 1989 as a manifestation of Romanianism which, for its own purposes, had to be equated with democracy. In Romania proper, however, few were those who had any clear notion what democracy meant or entailed since they had little experience, if any, with it in their lifetime, chiefly because they had lived under dictatorships for nearly half-a-century and had been isolated from the democratic world for at least four decades. And fewer yet were those who had recollections of pre-World War II Romanian democracy. All this is to say that, in fact, democracy was not a significant component of Romania's historic and political traditions.

The absence of that component is hardly surprising. The legitimacy of the Greater Romanian state, established at the end of World War I, was derived from nationalism. According to political leaders and the vast majority of Romanian intellectuals, past and present, the historic goal of all Romanians since the fifteenth century has been the liberation from foreign oppressors who had held the people in subjugation throughout the territories inhabited by Romanians. These oppressors have been identified as the Ottoman Turks and their surrogates, the Phanariote Greeks, in the Romanian provinces of Wallachia and Moldavia, the Magyars who ruled in

Transylvania, and the Russians who incorporated Bessarabia into what was perceived as the ever-threatening Russian empire.

The "struggle for liberation" and eventual unification of all Romanians under foreign rule or domination began in earnest in the nineteenth century, chiefly under the impact of the French Revolution and Napoleonic wars which inspired nationalist manifestations among Romanian leaders and intellectuals in Moldavia and Wallachia and, to a lesser degree, in Transylvania. The most virulent manifestations, such as the unsuccessful revolutions of 1821 and 1848, occurred in Moldavia and Wallachia - the component provinces of the small Romanian national state established in the 1860s which became the independent "Old Kingdom" in 1877. However, the "French connection" had little to do with the ideas of the French Revolution or those of French democracy, despite the fact that France was the source of inspiration and support for Francophile Romanian nationalists. To Romanian nationalists, mostly younger members of the Wallachian and Moldavian aristocracy, France was a fellow-Latin country which shared a common bond with the oppressed Romanians through Latinity as well as through common opposition to Russian domination over the Romanian provinces. To the future leaders of Romania, however, French democracy as such had no meaning; for them, the elimination of Russian and Ottoman influence did not entail the emancipation of the peasantry or the undertaking of social and political reforms of the French variety. It is true that the political platforms of the leaders of the revolutions of 1848 included provisions for furthering human and civil rights, but the prevalent political and socio-economic order was to remain intact except that political power was to be exercised almost exclusively by the younger rather than the older members of the aristocracy. Even in defeat, and in exile in France, the leaders of the failed revolutions paid only lip service to democratic reform as the continuing rationale for their own political existence was the rallying of support, in Romania and abroad, for the "struggle for independence" from onerous Turkish suzerainty and Russian domination. Thus, when as a consequence of international conflicts and diplomatic realignments, over which the Romanians had virtually no control, it was decided by the European Powers first to allow the unification of Moldavia and Wallachia into a Romanian state and later to recognize Romania's independence in 1878, the nationalist of Moldavia and Wallachia attained at least part of their historic goal through the creation of a small independent national state.

What is relevant to the topic of this paper was the *pro forma* acceptance, but *de facto* rejection, by Romanian political leaders of conditions for democratization of the Romanian political and social order imposed by the Powers as the price for international recognition of the Romanian state. Thus, unlike its Belgian prototype, the Constitution of 1866 limited the Romanians' civil and political rights while denying them altogether to the Jewish inhabitants of the country. In fact, the Jewish question became a key element in the recognition by the Powers of Romania's independence and it was only under duress that Romanian political leaders agreed, in extremis and mostly in bad faith, to grant basic civil rights to Jews without, however, allowing them to acquire citizenship. By itself this may not seem significant; however, in the context of nationalism and the corollary legitimacy of the national Romanian state, it assumed critical importance.

The nationalists' opposition to the wishes of the Powers was based on the view that even though the Powers could make all decisions regarding Romania's independence and borders, that independence was gained in 1877 by force of arms through the Romanians' successful participation in the Russo-Turkish War of 1877-78. To them, that war, fought by Romanians for Romanian independence, represented the triumph of the historic aspirations of the Romanians. Whereas such arguments are tenable in terms of Romanian nationalist doctrine, they merely revealed the fundamental incompatibility between that nationalism and western democracy. Indeed, the forerunners of independent Romania, identified as heroic Romanian princes of the past who fought bravely against foreign enemies, were not identifiable with anything but autocracy. Rulers such as Stephen the Great or Michael the Brave were symbolized as defenders of Romanian Orthodox Christianity and leaders of the people even though they were *primus inter pares* of the feudal oligarchic rule albeit exercised through parliament and political parties, remained the paramount feature of the political order of the Old Kingdom until the end of World War I.

Political life in the Old Kingdom focused on the peasant question which could not be resolved because of resistance by the landed aristocracy to redistribution of the country's wealth through a major land reform. Since the peasant question defied resolution, the battle cry of political leaders and nationalist intellectuals became the uniting of Romanians under foreign rule within the borders of a Great Romanian state. In its more extreme manifestations, the struggle for triumphant Romanianism assumed the form of an Orthodox Christian crusade which would rally the

Romanian masses against all enemies, domestic and foreign. This populism entailed virulent anti-Semitism since the Jews were regarded as exploiters of the Romanian people because of their economic activities as well as unassimilated non-Christian foreigners with no ties to Romanian culture and national interests. It also reinforced the anti-Hungarian and anti-Russian rhetoric related to the oppression of Romanians in Transylvania and Bessarabia, respectively.

Such views and actions augured badly for the future of democracy in a Greater Romanian state since democracy would entail recognition of the rights of ethnic and religious minorities and, above all, reconciliation of significantly different social, cultural, and economic values and experiences within the body politic of that state. Such considerations were, in fact, of major significance to political leaders in Transylvania and Bessarabia who were contemplating union with the Old Kingdom in the years of crisis antedating World War I.

There was no democratic tradition in the Romanian communities in Transylvania by the beginning of the twentieth century primarily because the dominant Hungarian political systems and its institutions were, *de facto*, democratic in name only. Nevertheless, while the Romanians' political and civil rights were severely curtailed by policies determined by Budapest and by the Hungarian aristocracy in Transylvania, it is true that the Romanian middle class did participate in the political life of the Austro-Hungarian monarchy as members of political parties with specific representation in the Hungarian parliament, with well defined civil rights, and with control over the political life of Romanian communities. However, as second class citizens, the majority of the Romanian population, still primarily agricultural, was subject to discrimination by Hungarian officialdom in matters cultural and administrative. Nevertheless, the Romanian leaders had a different political mentality and goals than those of the Old Kingdom. Since the leadership consisted of representatives of the intellectual, clerical, and commercial groups in the absence of a Romanian landed aristocracy in Transylvania, and since the Romanian peasantry generally owned land and enjoyed greater prosperity than that of the Old Kingdom, the Romanian communities were much more socially and politically homogeneous than those of the neo-feudal Romanian state. Moreover, nationalism in Transylvania was basically directed against the Hungarian political leaders and bureaucracy rather than against Jews and other non-Romanian minorities. Indeed, the Romanians' political culture and socio-economic interests reflected the realities of their historic experience in the Habsburg empire which was indeed different from that of their co-nationals in Moldavia and Wallachia. Paternalism, from the level of the emperor to that of local political and religious leaders, was as integral a part of the political culture as "bourgeois" values and aspirations were integral parts of their existence and desiderata.

The political platforms of nationalist Transylvanian political leaders sought first and foremost the retention of the cultural values of the Romanians, whether Orthodox or Uniate, and the expansion of their property rights through acquisition of land and increased opportunities in urban economic and professional activities. And all these desiderata were to be realized through the instrumentality of political parties representative of the interests of the Romanian communities within the framework of a parliamentary system. As such, Transylvanian Romanianism was compatible with a potentially democratic order in a Greater Romanian state.

This was hardly true of the political tradition of the Romanians of Bessarabia. As a border province of Russia, Bessarabia was a Jewish pale as well as a territory inhabited by Romanian peasants and intellectuals, Russian bureaucrats and military personnel, and a large number of smaller ethnic minorities. Russian democracy, even in its rudimentary forms in effect after the Revolution of 1905, had little impact on Bessarabia. The Romanian nationalist leaders, mostly intellectuals, as well as the Romanian peasantry, were distinctly less anti-Russian than anti-Semitic since the province's economic activities and urban life were dominated by Jews. Romanian nationalist leaders favored integration into a Greater Romania but, realistically, that possibility could be entertained only during World War I. In the absence of any Romanian political party and clear opposition to secession by all Russian governments, including the Bolshevik before the end of World War I, political experience in anything but authoritarian, if not always anti-democratic, organizations was unknown. Integration into Greater Romania became possible only after the collapse of the tsarist regime. The threat posed to the interests of the Romanian nationalist political leaders and the wealthier peasantry by Bolshevik policies which entailed redistribution of wealth and utilization of the Jewish pale for Lenin's political purposes precipitated the Romanian unionist actions at a time of political turmoil in Russia. However, the Bessarabian political leadership, whose Romanianism was more of a reaction to Judeo-Bolshevism than a commitment to the nationalist cause of the Old Kingdom, sought to insure the interests of the Bessarabians through a politically representative system which would guarantee their property and political rights.

It is uncertain whether Romanianism as such would have been a sufficiently unifying bond for the Romanian people had the unification occurred under circumstances different than those present in 1919. In 1918, with the defeat of the Austro-Hungarian monarchy and the collapse of the Russian empire, whatever guarantees would have been sought by Transylvanian and Bessarabian leaders in prolonged negotiations with the rulers of the Old Kingdom were not obtainable. The Old Kingdom, which joined the victorious allies in 1916, became by default the core of Greater Romania and its leaders assumed the role of "unifiers" of all Romanians and executors of the Romanian historic legacy. And the state thus created was to be ruled by, and in the interest of, the leaders of the Old Kingdom whose propensities for democracy were at best marginal.

It has been argued by parties interested in depicting interwar Romanian politics, and the Greater Romanian state, as democratic that unequivocal compliance with the democratic principles imposed upon Greater Romania by the victorious allies as the price for recognition of its legitimacy would have been impractical under the conditions prevailing at the end of World War I. Nationalist historians and politicians and their acolytes at home and abroad have pretended, and still pretend, that most of the essential features of democracy were acceptable to the Romanian political leaders at the end of World War I and were, in fact, present in interwar Romania prior to the establishment of the royal dictatorship in 1938. Specifically, it is suggested that acceptance of the conditions imposed by the allies - to wit, party pluralism, freedom of speech, press and assembly, respect for human, civil and minority rights, toleration of religious and ethnic diversity, and a democratic constitution - were in fact compatible with the democratic proclivities of the Romanian people and their leaders. If not all prerequisites could always be implemented it was because of "objective" domestic and international conditions which required alterations, albeit "exceptional," for protecting the national interest. But these contentions are questionable.

From the very inception of Greater Romania, the Bucharest political oligarchy, headed by the Bratianu family and its National Liberal Party, viewed itself not only as the fulfiller of the national historic legacy but also as its executor. In short, it was "Romania for the Romanians," but led by the Romanians of the Old Kingdom who were the unifiers. To them, Greater Romania was greater prewar Romania. Yet the political problems of the Old Kingdom were compounded following the incorporation of Transylvania and Bessarabia in 1918. Greater Romania had to address minority questions related to the Hungarians and Germans of Transylvania and, by extension, to deal with the irredentism of a Hungary irreconcilable over the loss of Transylvania. It also had to face a hostile and revisionist Bolshevik Russia which refused to recognize the loss of Bessarabia and encouraged revolutionary activities in that province. Moreover, it had to address the peasant and corollary questions on a broad national basis.

The Bucharest oligarchy, which had agreed to the undertaking of a major land reform in the Old Kingdom only in the face of the threat of a communist-inspired peasant uprising at the end of the war, sought to limit its scope at the end of the conflict. This was primarily because in the predominantly agrarian Old Kingdom, the power elite comprised primarily the landed aristocracy whose loss of land could only be tolerated if it meant retention of political power. However, in postwar Romania the threat to that power was to come from the Transylvanian political leadership whose own power was based on the support of the wealthier, better educated, and truly emancipated Romanian peasantry as well as from an urban intellectual and merchant class. Inasmuch as the National Party of Transylvania, with its large peasant constituency, had common interests with the post-1918 Peasant Party of the Old Kingdom, means had to be found by the Bratianus and their allies to prevent the transfer of power, through free democratic elections, to peasant-supported parties. It is for this reason, then, that acceptance by the Bucharest political leadership of the imposed requirements of political pluralism and free elections were more formal than real.

More indicative yet of the sincerity of Bucharest's commitment to allied-imposed democracy was the virulent initial opposition to the granting of political and citizenship rights to Jews and acceptance of external supervision of the enactment and enforcement of imposed minority rights.

Opposition to the granting of rights to the Jewish population has been generally interpreted as rejection of external interference in the internal affairs of a sovereign national state. Thus, Ioan I. C. Bratianu, as leader of the Liberal Party and chief negotiator at the Paris Peace Conference, would not accept the "humiliating conditions" which closely resembled those which, under similar pressure, had to be at least *pro forma* accepted in 1878 by the Old Kingdom. But this explanation is rather simplistic even though it is partially accurate. The political rights of the Jews were closely related to minority rights and to the very legitimacy of triumphant Romanian nationalism and the national state. Moldavians and Bessarabians had always regarded Jews as a foreign element in the body social and cultural. The reincorporation of Bessarabia into historic Moldavia greatly increased the size of a largely non-Romanian-speaking Jewish population concentrated in the towns of these provinces. To Romanian nationalists, the Jews not only were non-participants in the realization of nationalist goals but, after 1917, they were also regarded as pro-, if not outright supportive of, Bolshevism and its anti-Romanian goals. Thus, the extending of political rights to Jews was doubly unacceptable. As an additional argument against recognition of Jews as citizens, Ioan I. C. Bratianu tied the Jews not only to Bolshevism and Russian irredentism, but also to Bolshevism and Hungarian irredentism since the Hungarian Communist Republic, established in 1919 by Béla Kun, presented not only a threat to the security of all of Eastern Europe, in view of its ties to Lenin, but also because of its specific threat to Transylvania. Since Kun was a Jew and most of his followers were also Jewish, and since Bessarabian Jews were viewed as pro-communist and supportive of Russian revisionism, Bratianu posited himself as the defender of Eastern Europe against the "Judeo-Bolshevik conspiracy" in general and against Romania and Romanian nationalism in particular. By extension then, while willing to protect the rights of the Hungarian minority in Transylvania, he would not tolerate external intervention on behalf of that minority since that minority was sympathetic, if not necessarily to Bolshevism, certainly to Hungarian irredentism.

Whereas these contentions were plausible and, in certain instances, also correct, Bratianu's reluctant acceptance of the requirements for democratization of Greater Romania by the victorious powers allowed for circumvention since at least France, for its own strategic and political interests, sought Romania's support for the establishment of the anti-Bolshevik and anti-German *Cordon Sanitaire* in Eastern Europe. In fact, the much acclaimed, nowadays, "democratic" Constitution of 1923 contained sufficient loopholes to allow avoidance of implementation of certain provisions in cases of national emergency.

Formally, Romania became a constitutional democracy - or rather a constitutional monarchy with a democratic constitution - in 1923. In practice, however, constitutionalism did not engender genuine democracy. It is fair to say that basic freedoms and civil and political rights were guaranteed and exercised by the population. It is also fair to say that party pluralism was in existence and that many political parties had genuinely democratic platforms and programs. However, only the National Peasant Party was able to assume power in the late 1920s and try to implement its principles, albeit with limited success, during a short time in office. Other democratically-oriented political organizations, chiefly the Social Democratic Party, could never hope to take office partly because of the lack of a significant constituency, given the small size of the industrial working class and of its illegitimacy - on both nationalist and ideological grounds - in the eyes of nationalist politicians, but also because of the customary manipulation of the electoral process and falsification of results by the parties in power. Indeed, electoral fraud was so blatant in interwar Romania that the governing party in one year, on the basis of the having secured over 75 percent of the votes presumably cast in its favor, could - and on occasion did - secure less than 10 percent of the ballots cast in the election immediately following.

It is true that such abuses were less prevalent when the National Liberal Party, controlled by the Bratianus, was in power during most of the 1920s and certainly so during the governance of the National Peasant Party. However, other means contrary to constitutional provisions were used by the Bratianus to secure their stranglehold on power. Thus, in keeping with their claims to legitimacy as defenders of the national interest, they outlawed the Romanian Communist Party, the ostensible tool of the "Judeo-Bolshevik conspiracy," in 1924. Similarly, they used dilatory and obfuscatory tactics to prevent implementation of the minority treaties, invoking, often justifiably, the irredentism of the Hungarians. Most significantly in the long run, however, they tolerated if not encouraged the activities of overtly anti-democratic and virulently anti-Semitic, xenophobic, and ultra-nationalist political organizations such as the League of National Christian Defense or the Legion of the Archangel Michael, the forerunner of the fascist Iron Guard of later years.

Nevertheless, despite these questionable exercises of "democratic" power, the provisions of the Constitution of 1923 were at least formally adhered to until 1930. It was in that year, and specifically with the accession to the Romanian throne of King Carol II, that the end of democracy was supposedly in sight.

It has become fashionable among historians and survivors of the political arena of the interwar years to hold Carol II responsible for the decline and eventual collapse of democracy in Romania. The essence of this most questionable contention is the presumption that the King nurtured royal absolutism from the moment he "usurped" the throne upon his illegal return from political exile in September 1930. Whereas it is true that Carol never forgave the Bratianus for forcing him to relinquish his right of succession to the throne because of his morganatic marriage in the 1920s and that he was contemptuous of the Romanian political system, it is also true that Carol's return to Romania was engineered by political leaders who were persuaded that political stability could be better assured by Carol than by bickering political parties and an ineffectual regency acting on behalf of the nine year old King Michael.

The belief, held by many political leaders and by much of the population at large, that stability could be restored in times of crisis by a stronger leader - in Romania's case, by the King - was as evident in 1930 as it is today. For indeed, neither the National Liberal nor the National Peasant parties - the so-called "historic parties" - were able to find adequate solutions to the economic, social, and political problems of Romania during their years of governance. Those failures were not so much due to adherence or non-adherence to democratic principles or practices as to the economic and social realities of a country faced with the consequences of transition from a predominantly agricultural society to an industrial one. The transition was particularly difficult, at least politically, because modernization entailed displacement of the overwhelmingly Romanian Orthodox population to urban centers different in culture, mentality, and even language. This was particularly the case in Moldavia, Transylvania, and Bucharest because the great majority of the Jewish population was urban and the Jews, together with the Hungarians, Germans, and other ethnically diverse city dwellers, were dominant in economic, cultural, and professional activities related to modernization. This situation resulted in virulent anti-Semitic and xenophobic manifestations by frustrated students and workers in Moldavia and, to a lesser degree, in Transylvania and Wallachia, and to opposition by nationalist politicians to foreign investment in the Romanian economy. In fact, the National Liberal Party, in the 1920s, by virtue of its self-determined mandate as protector and executor of the Romanian nationalist legacy decreed that modernization had to be achieved "by ourselves" so as to avoid external interference in the conduct of Romanian affairs. By contrast, the National Peasant Party favored international investment, opposed xenophobic and anti-Semitic manifestations, sought improvement in the economic status of the peasantry and of the working class, and applied these principles during its brief period of governance. However, inherited problems could not be resolved in the early stages of the Great Depression as the world economic crisis began to affect even the underdeveloped Romanian economy. And the resultant disaffection and malaise of the rural and urban population led to increased popular support for the pro-fascist political Right and, to a lesser extent, the pro-Stalinist Left. Thus, to many, King Carol was to solve problems which could be blamed on internal policies and foreign developments which he neither formulated nor influenced and which often defied democratic solutions.

It would be difficult to deny that Carol's concept of the role of a constitutional monarch was closer to that of Napoleon III than to those of contemporary Scandinavian monarchs. But his views and actions were fully compatible with those of King Carol I and, in a broader historic perspective, with those of the revered Romanian medieval princes so dear to Romanian nationalist leaders. It is true that he strengthened the power of the monarchy which had been virtually nil during the regential regime. In fact, it was precisely the reaffirmation of the constitutional rights of the monarchy that incurred the hostility of the political oligarchy that had in effect replaced the king as the ultimate arbiter of political problems, upholder of the constitution, and defender of national integrity. It is true that Carol II manipulated the political process by exceeding the customary royal prerogative of dissolving parliament and then selecting prime ministers unrepresentative of the popular will who, through habitual electoral fraud, could form a government subservient to the monarch. It is also true that he surrounded himself with what was broadly viewed as a camarilla of unsavory politicians and advisers including, to the dismay of conservatives and nationalists, his Jewish mistress, Elena Lupescu. However, except for the exercising of powers previously reserved to political oligarchies, which engendered their hostility, the monarch would have acted on much firmer ground had he not incurred the wrath of respected political leaders such as the head of the National Peasant Party, Iuliu Maniu, and of the nationalist Right and radical Right because of the political and personal presence of Elena Lupescu.

As it turned out, his Achilles' heel was not adherence or non-adherence to constitutional and/or democratic practices since the King did not exceed his constitutional prerogatives nor did he try to revoke the fundamental democratic rights of the citizenry, interfere with the freedom of the press and religion, restrict minority rights, or limit political pluralism prior to 1938. His contribution to the decline and eventual demise of democratic forces in Romania was indirect and expressly related to factors related to the evolution of the power of the anti-democratic, pro-, and later, fascist Romanian extremist political Right.

The nature and significance of the political Right of the pre-communist period has been subject to massive reinterpretation in recent years. Nowadays, the leaders of extremist organizations or governments such as Corneliu Zelea Codreanu, the "Führer" of the Iron Guard, Marshal Ion Antonescu, the wartime dictator of Romania, Octavian Goga, the co-leader of the virulently anti-Semitic Goga-Cuza government that preceded the establishment of the royal dictatorship in 1938, are often being depicted as great patriots, exponents of true Romanianism, and in some instances, if not necessarily champions of democracy, at least as genuine closet democrats. Except for the opportunistic and hilariously absurd "democratization" of the radical Right, there can be little doubt that it played a major role in Romanian political life in the interwar years, that it reflected the mentality, passions, and prejudices of a significant segment of the population, and that it was fundamentally opposed to democracy in both theory and practice.

The equally popular argument that the evolution of the extreme Right in the 1930s was related to its determination to cleanse the Romanian body politic and social from the corruption characteristic of the rule of Carol II and of his camarilla and associates, which included the Jewess Elena Lupescu and other Jews or Judaizers, albeit by legal and constitutional means, is just as untenable as that of finding an organic connection between Right wing nationalism and authoritarianism and democracy. The fact is that from its very inception, the extremist Right opposed modernization, democratization, toleration of ethnic, religious, and cultural diversity as alien and inimical to the Orthodox Romanian historic national tradition and future.

To the extreme Right, the ultimate enemies were the Jews and the Bolsheviks who, in its view, shared the same anti-Christian ideology and anti-Romanianism. The Jews, moreover, as urban capitalists in Romania, were branded as the blood-suckers of the Romanian peasantry and controllers of the economic and social evolution of the Romanian people. It is indeed noteworthy that the most famous organizations of the radical Right shared a common origin and ideology. The League of National Christian Defense (LANC) was created by A. C. Cuza, a professor at the University of Iasi, and the Legion of the Archangel Michael was an offspring of Cuza's organization, set up by his disciples who found the mere anti-Semitism of Cuza's ideology too narrow for their Christian populist concerns. And therein lies the difference that led to the eventual success of the Legion.

While the Legion, headed by Corneliu Zelea Codreanu, shared Cuza's anti-Semitism and anti-Bolshevism, it was less elitist in its composition. Cuza was an urban intellectual; the members of the Legion were largely sons of emancipated peasants who, as students and urban dwellers, resented the dominance of the Jewish bourgeoisie with its virtual monopoly on economic and professional activities in Moldavia. The members of the Legion had the distinct advantage of direct communication with the village, with the urban Romanian proletariat, and with fellow students including those attending or having graduated from theological seminaries, who either were, or could directly recruit, members of the rural or urban clergy for activist, populist, Orthodox Romanianism.

The Christian, Orthodox, populist nationalism so characteristic of the Legion had limited appeal for the Romanian peasantry in the early postwar years as the peasants were supportive, if not necessarily of democracy, at least of what they considered to be their best political representative, the National Peasant Party. It was only after the agrarian crisis related to the great Depression affected the peasantry adversely that inroads could be, and were, made by the Legion and even by the LANC who blamed the peasants' despondency on Jewish capitalism and on the presumed Judeo-Bolshevik conspiracy directed against Romanian Orthodox society. It was also then that the Legion made further inroads in urban centers as the economic crisis affected the working class and the petty bourgeoisie both ready to accept the conspiracy theories advanced by the radical Right.

The exploitation of the national and international crises of the thirties by the Legion and its political sympathizers gained momentum with the worsening of the economic crisis at home and with the rise in Hitler's and Stalin's power. Political assassinations, which were part of the League's arsenal against its enemies, were depicted as symbolic of the spirit of sacrifice of true believers in the Christian national renaissance; participation in the Spanish Civil War on the side of the nationalists was heralded as the League's readiness to sacrifice its best sons in the struggle against heathen Judeo-Bolshevism.

Whereas prior to 1936 direct or indirect support of the League from sympathizers was lukewarm, it became pronounced in that year and the following as significant segments of the Romanian population applauded the League's ostensibly selfless commitment to ridding the world, and Romania particularly, of what the ignorant, disgruntled, or prejudiced believed to be a genuine threat from Judeo-Bolshevism. The national Christian crusade against Bolshevism and its presumed representatives in Romania, the

Jewish-dominated, illegal Left and its supporters, the Jewish-dominated press, not to mention the ostensibly pro-communist trade unions and the unassimilated and presumably anti-Romanian majority of the Jewish population in general, gained momentum in the crucial year for democracy's survival in Romania - 1937, the year when national elections were to be held.

There is general agreement among students of Romanian history and political that the elections of December 1937 were the only truly free elections in interwar Romania and, as such, a test of Romanian democracy. It is also generally agreed that the results of the elections were such as to pave the way to the collapse of the democratic order in 1938 with the establishment of the royal dictatorship in February of that year. But there is continuing controversy over the responsibility for the discontinuation of the democratic experiment, albeit in its Romanian form, with the majority of contemporary nationalist political leaders and their surrogates - nationalist historians, journalists, and propagandists - laying the blame more on King Carol II than on the radical Right and its political allies. The controversy is relevant only for assessing the prospects for the future of democracy in contemporary, post-Ceausescu Romania since only the most cynical, opportunistic, and partisan analysts of the politics of late interwar Romania could attribute any democratic proclivities to the radical Right.

Throughout 1937 and beyond, the Legion expressed its support for Hitler's domestic and foreign policies and disdain for parliamentary democracy. It is also noteworthy that Codreanu himself, as well as the organization in general, were not puppets of Hitler, nor were they financed by Nazi Germany to any meaningful extent. The Legion's participation in the electoral process was not related to any commitment to that process; rather, it was intended to prevent the victory of the ruling National Liberal Party which was clearly identified with the despised royal establishment. The same electoral goal, albeit primarily because of the anti-Carol sentiments, was shared by the leader of the principal democratic opposition party, Iuliu Maniu. Despite his credentials as a genuine believer in democratic rule, Maniu committed the grave error of concluding an electoral pact with Codreanu in the expectation that the Romanian peasantry, which represented the vast majority of the electorate, would cast enough votes to prevent the election of the National Liberal Party and presumably, because of the electoral alliance, it would vote for either the Legion or the National Peasant Party in sufficient numbers to insure the plurality required for victory for Maniu's party. Whereas it may be possible to attribute Maniu's alliance with Codreanu to a common desire to rid Romania of political corruption, it is obvious that Maniu was willing to choose between two evils by collaborating with an overtly anti-democratic, if not yet outright fascist, organization at the risk of discrediting his own commitment to democratic rule.

As for the King's commitment to democracy, there can be little doubt that he would have maintained at least a democratic façade had the National Liberal, or even the National Peasant, Party won the election. Despite his authoritarian tendencies and exercise of power through his camarilla and National Liberal government of his choice, Carol was genuinely opposed to Hitler, Mussolini, and Stalin and struggled to maintain Romania's political ties with France and England. Dictatorial rule would have been counterproductive as it would have jeopardized the credibility of his allegiance to western democratic opponents to dictatorship. It is not that Carol was unaware of the danger posed to the National Liberals by the electoral alliance of Maniu and Codreanu but, like most political leaders, he was unaware of the strength of the Romanian radical Right in 1937.

The results of the election of December 1937, if anything, proved that the Romanians' commitment to democracy was not very profound. The Legion's party, "All for the Fatherland," received 16 percent of the popular vote and the Goga-Cuza coalition about 9 percent. It is believed that the percentage of votes obtained by the Legion would have been higher had it not been for the electoral alliance with Maniu's party. In fact, the National Peasant Party refused to accept the King's mandate to form a new government following the defeat of the National Liberals, ostensibly because of its opposition to Carol's *modus operandi* but, in reality, because of its realization that without a majority in parliament, it would have to cooperate with the radical Right which would compromise its own principles. The electoral results revealed the effectiveness of nationalist, xenophobic, and, above all, anti-Semitic and anti-communist propaganda disseminated by the radical Right. The Legion made extravagant promises to the peasantry by guaranteeing ownership of land to all peasants through expropriation, confiscation, and redistribution of Jewish wealth. Similar promises were made to the impoverished urban proletariat who would share in that wealth. The profoundly anti-Semitic rhetoric was accompanied by equally radical attacks against anti-Romanian foreigners, most notably Hungarian irredentists abroad and in Romania, the revisionist Russian Bolshevik empire, the Judaizers in the King's entourage, and all misguided Romanian socialists, intellectuals, and compromisers with alien values and ideologies. In sum, the Legion posited itself as the ultimate exponent of grass roots Romanianism who could best defend and advance the security of a country exploited by Jews and menaced by communists and foreign irredentists.

Perhaps less effective in its propaganda, which limited itself primarily to the Jewish menace and its extirpation, the Goga-Cuza coalition also scored heavily in regions with large urban Jewish enclaves. And, in the last analysis, most political parties stressed their commitment to the defense of the country against foreign enemies and to Romanian nationalism. Few indeed were the politicians who based their campaigns on commitment to democratic institutions and practices and the parties of those who did obtained collectively less than 10 percent of the total votes cast.

Under the circumstances, the King asked the fourth highest vote-getting organization, the Goga-Cuza coalition, to form a new government. He could not offer the mandate to the National Liberals who lost the election; the National Peasant Party refused to accept it; the Legion was too radical, too committed to Hitler and the destruction of royal power for him to do so. Carol was fully aware of the new government's anti-democratic platform and programs; in fact, it is generally correctly assumed that he sought to compromise the radical Right with a view to replacing the government not with a democratic one, but with one headed by himself as the savior of the nation and the national interest from actual or potential enemies from within or without Greater Romania. The planned royal dictatorship was to seek a "Romanian renascence" which would insure political stability and defense of Romania's national interests.

The royal dictatorship was authoritarian rather than fascist. Carol's main opponent, the Iron Guard, regarded it as insufficiently repressive of Jewish interests, too tolerant of Hungarian irredentism, too compromising with Bolshevism, and too disinterested in cooperating with Germany in matters political and economic. On the other hand, with few notable exceptions, Romanian political leaders joined the so-called "Front of National Renascence" and collaborated with the King's camarilla in the common goal of preserving the integrity of Greater Romania. Thus, the political dialogue and confrontations after February 1938 no longer involved pro- and anti-democratic forces but confrontations between the fascist, totalitarian Iron Guard and the authoritarian royal dictatorship. The outcome of the struggle for power was ultimately resolved in favor of the Iron Guard when, following the forced abdication of King Carol II in the fall of 1940, the royal dictatorship was replaced by that of General Ion Antonescu and the Iron Guard who became rulers of the National Legionary Romanian state.

Whereas a discussion of pre-communist dictatorships may seem irrelevant to an assessment of the evolution of Romanian democracy since 1938, it is fair to say that now, as claims of democratic continuity even during so-called periods of dictatorship are so abundant, it is imperative to assess the accuracy of such assertions.

Inasmuch as King Carol and his closest associates and advisers are no longer alive, and since many of the leading members of the Front of National Renascence supported Antonescu's dictatorship, it has become necessary for those interested in demonstrating the continuity of a democratic tradition, albeit under authoritarian rule, that Antonescu's dictatorship was not "fascist" but merely an authoritarian, military one, unavoidable under the circumstances prevailing in Romania in late 1940. Antonescu's pro-western and early democratic convictions are stressed and his revulsion over Carol's violation of democratic principles and practices are supposed to account for Antonescu's belief that authoritarian rule was required to restore order and stability and to defend the Romanian national interest against Bolshevism.

Similarly, surviving members of the Iron Guard and their disciples have claimed, at least since the end of World War II, that their ideology and political philosophy were not incompatible with democracy. In fact, according to them, the Legion was readying itself for participation in the national elections which, according to the Constitution of 1923, had to take place in 1938 and it was precisely because of the King's fear of a Legionary victory that he abolished parliament and sought annihilation of the Iron Guard. The Legion's political radicalism has also been reinterpreted to the extent that its virulent anti-Semitism did not contemplate the violation of the civil and political rights of Jews as long as those rights were to be exercised in Palestine. In fact, as proof of these democratic sentiments, defenders of the Legion emphasize its slogan, "Jews in Palestine."

Whereas such arguments are blatantly absurd with respect to the Guard's democratic inclinations, it is important to note that Carol's decision to annihilate the Iron Guard was based on his conviction that Codreanu and his cohorts were likely to make further converts among the urban and rural youth and that their influence in villages and particularly in the armed forces would continue to grow. Thus, the Guard posed a clear danger to the King's own political survival. The radical measures taken against the leadership, culminating in the assassinations of Corneliu Zelea Codreanu and his close associates, presumably with Carol's consent if not on his express orders, in 1938 turned out to be counterproductive. The legionaries, bent on revenge, soon resorted to political assassination and beatings of perceived enemies while seeking to exploit the political opportunities created by international events that undermined the royal dictatorship. The cession, under the threat of military action, of Bessarabia and Northern Bukovina to the Soviet Union in June 1940, the loss of Northern Transylvania to Hungary through the so-called Vienna Diktat in August of that year, and the corollary cession of Southern Dobrudja to Bulgaria in September, were all blamed by the Iron Guard and its supporters in the armed forces on the King's inability to defend the cause of Romanianism in the spirit and manner best exemplified by the great national heroes of the past and their legitimate successors, most notably Corneliu Zelea Codreanu and General Ion Antonescu. Thus, in the absence of Codreanu, the national honor and eventual restoration of Greater Romania for Romanians was to be entrusted to the valiant Antonescu and his fellow legionaries who could best mobilize the nation for the realization of its betrayed historic goals.

The attribution, *ex post facto*, of democratic intentions or convictions to the leaders of the Antonescu-Guardist dictatorship is senseless even if, presumably, their ostensible commitment to democracy had to be temporarily abandoned for the sake of facilitating the eventual realization of the Romanians' historic goals - goals frustrated by foreign and domestic enemies identified, in 1940 as throughout the interwar years, as international and national communism and Judaism and, to an almost equal extent, Hungarian irredentism. But what is remarkable in the context of assessment of Romanian political culture is the fact that the vast majority of the Romanian people supported the new dictatorship. It certainly agreed with its nationalist goals if not with its pro-Nazi and overtly anti-Semitic policies. And perhaps even more noteworthy is the collaboration of political leaders of the Carolist dictatorship with that of Antonescu, albeit often justified in terms of a common commitment to the national interest.

The political opposition to Antonescu's dictatorship, particularly after Romania joined the war against the Soviet Union in June 1941, came primarily from anti-Antonescu, radical legionaries who took refuge in Germany and Austria after the failure of the so-called Legionary Revolution, directed and crushed by Antonescu in January 1941, and from several prewar lesser political figures with genuine democratic convictions, mostly members of the diplomatic service who resigned in protest over the establishment of the dictatorship and remained abroad after September 1940. Inside the country, non-collaboration with the regime has been interpreted as evidence of tacit democratic opposition to "fascism." This diagnosis is correct with respect to leaders and members of minor, powerless political organizations of the interwar years or of the historic parties whose influence in party affairs had never been paramount. However, it is also true that even among those political and military leaders who collaborated with Antonescu's dictatorship, generally because of a common commitment to the restoration of Greater Romania and corollary anti-Magyarism and anti-Bolshevism, there were men who were uneasy about the dictatorship. But it would erroneous to attribute the opposition to Antonescu's rule, which became manifest in the later stages of Romania's disastrous war against the Soviet Union and which resulted in the overthrow of the dictatorship through the so-called "royal coup d'état" of August 1944, to previously hidden, lifelong commitments to democracy.

The significance of the overthrow of Antonescu's dictatorship in the evaluation of the realities - past, present, and future - of the "Romanian road to democracy" is unmistakable. It has generally been represented as an expression of Romanian rejection of "fascism" and a commitment to democracy. It is now recognized that the decision to arrest Antonescu and shift sides in the waning stages of World War II by joining the victorious allies was engineered by the entourage of King Michael with the consent of the monarch. Yet that action, and the ensuing support of the Romanian armed forces, of leaders of revived political parties, and of the vast majority of the Romanian people for the decision to join the western allies was motivated more by the fear of a military takeover of Romania by the rapidly advancing Red Army than by either a rejection of Antonescu's goals or by an irrevocable commitment to democracy. In fact, it was hoped that Romania's military actions against their former allies would, by accelerating the defeat of the Nazi forces in Eastern Europe, secure the restitution of the territories lost by Romania in 1940.

Unfortunately, as it turned out, professions of commitment to democracy and opposition to dictatorships, "fascist" or "communist," failed to persuade the cynical British and American war leaders of the sincerity of the Romanians' representations. Instead, they accepted at face value Stalin's assurances of restoring democracy in Romania.

It is evident in retrospect that the western allies were not impressed by Stalin's commitment to "non-interference in Romanian internal affairs," as ostensibly demonstrated by the participation of Romanian communists in the anti-fascist actions of August 1944. Still, for tactical purposes, they did not challenge the validity of the contentions of the communists that the overthrow of Antonescu's dictatorship succeeded not on account of the palace coup, but because of an anti-fascist revolution of the Romanian people led by the only truly democratic force in Romania, the communists.

It is possible that in August 1944 the western allies, and even the Romanian communist or pro-communists leaders and followers who joined the anti-Nazi and anti-Soviet originators of the coup, believed that the democratization of postwar Romania would be feasible within a multiparty, parliamentary, democratic political system. But, even if they entertained such illusions, they were unaware of Stalin's definition of "democracy." Indeed, the road to "people's democracy," the euphemism for totalitarian dictatorship by the people's representative - the Stalinist communist party - was opened for all to see within weeks of Stalin's representatives and agents taking *de facto* control of the "democratization" of Romania.

During the few months that elapsed between August 1944 and March 1945, when a Stalinist-controlled coalition government assumed power in Romania, the previous coalition governments headed by the Romanian generals Sanatescu and Radescu did indeed undertake the dismantling of the Antonescu dictatorship. It is probable that had it not been for the provocations engineered by Stalinists in the revitalized Romanian Communist Party, with the support of the Red Army and Soviet officials stationed in Romania, the Sanatescu and Radescu governments could have paved the way to restoration of democracy in postwar Romania. However, that would have entailed at least partial satisfaction of the ultimate *raison d'être* of the coup of 1944: the elimination of the threat of Bolshevism and recovery of Northern Transylvania and, hopefully, also Bessarabia; in other words, the realization of the historic national goal of Greater Romania. That, however, could not have been accomplished without support from the western allies since Stalin's intentions toward Romania were evident to all concerned by 1945. It is noteworthy that Stalin catered to Romanian nationalism by returning Northern Transylvania to Romania within a few days after the installation of the communist-dominated coalition government headed by Petru Groza in March 1945. Still, the Groza government maintained enough of a democratic façade to persuade the essentially politically-naive or indifferent Romanian masses that communism was not incompatible with mass participation in political life and enjoyment of basic freedoms. It was only after the totally fraudulent elections of 1946 - the last multiparty elections in Romania for more than four decades - that the annihilation of opposition parties, the arrest and imprisonment of actual and potential opponents of Stalinism, and a general reign of terror directed against the Stalinist-defined "class enemy" began in earnest on the egregious assumption that legitimacy for the "socialist transformation" of Romania was secured by the people's free will. By the end of December 1947, following recognition at the Paris peace conference of a Stalinist regime by the United States and its allies, the monarchy was abolished and the Romanian People's Republic, a genuine "people's democracy," was formally set up. Totalitarianism was to last for exactly forty-two years.

Inasmuch as nobody has yet uncovered democratic elements in Romanian communist totalitarianism, it may well be asked who and where were the democratic or pro-democratic exponents of opposition to the regimes and policies of Nicolae Ceausescu and his predecessors?

There were some in Romania but, because of ruthless persecution of even moderately outspoken dissenters, the opposition to the dictatorship was, with minimal exceptions, passive. It manifested itself primarily through non-participation in organized pro-communist manifestations whenever possible, refusal to join the Communist Party, and avoidance of cooperation with the security police as informers. But these evasive tactics did not necessarily imply a commitment to democracy; rather, they generally were statements against the specific character of the communist dictatorship. In fact, politically-motivated opposition, albeit tacit, by pro-democratic Romanians was generally limited to urban intellectuals, frequently disenchanted idealists who had supported communism in the last stages of the war and early postwar period and were later expelled from the Party and often imprisoned for "Titoism" or similar ideological deviations from Stalinism. But such opposition was ineffectual partly because of the surveillance of intellectuals and politically-suspect former Party members by the secret police and also because of its constituency's inability to communicate with the masses. Still, since a few intellectuals did have contacts with the youth, primarily in the specialized higher educational system, they were able to influence students aware of the shortcomings of communism. In that respect, their impact on the younger generation was similar to that of the non-collaborationist members of the Romanian clergy. Even though the upper Orthodox hierarchy did cooperate, mostly by political necessity, with the communist dictatorship, members of the faculties of theology did, at least by innuendo, reflect on the incompatibility of communist and Christian tenets and values. However, since such members of the clergy were more concerned with inculcating Orthodox populism than democratic cosmopolitanism, they were regarded as a more serious threat to the communist order than the secular, non-nationalist, urban intellectuals.

The only meaningful, belatedly but ultimately successful, political opposition to Ceausescu's dictatorship was that of the once leading members of the upper Communist Party hierarchy which manifested itself openly only in 1989. These communists advocated renunciation of neo-Stalinism, economic reform, "socialism with a human face" and, in effect, the emulation of Gorbachev's *Perestroika* and *Glasnost*. It was not democratic in the western European sense; however, it was in favor of democratization of the "national socialism" of the Ceausescu era. It corresponded most closely to the desiderata and political culture of the population at large.

Overt political opposition to the communist dictatorship in Romania was feasible only outside the country itself by members of the Romanian political emigration. Such opposition did indeed exist. It was always anti-communist but not always pro-democracy. In fact, the most vocal and, eventually, the most influential opposition came from former members or sympathizers of the Iron Guard whose anti-communism was frequently equated with their self-proclaimed, long-standing commitment to democracy. That segment of the political opposition, activating primarily from Spain, Germany, and Latin America, where its members had taken refuge during or at the end of World War II, was reinforced by émigrés from communist Romania and focused chiefly on the incompatibility of communism and Orthodoxy, of communist nationalism and Orthodox nationalism; in other words, on juxtaposing populist Romanianism and communist Romanianism. Its *bête noire* was not only Ceausescu, whose nationalism through its anti-Hungarianism, anti-Russianism, and anti-Semitism resembled that of Antonescu and, except for its lack of Orthodoxy, also that of the Iron Guard but also, and primarily, communism per se, which continued to be viewed as a Judeo-Bolshevik, anti-Christian ideology introduced and enforced in Romania by Jews and Judaizers. The pretense of democracy was readily validated by anti-communist governments that chose to ignore the activists' nefarious anti-democratic past. Less active, less significant, and more committed to the eventual replacement of the communist dictatorship with a democratic regime were the political émigrés in the United States and England who were supported by the American and British governments.

Brought together under the aegis of the American-financed Romanian National Committee, well-known intellectuals, diplomats, and political leaders - mostly with genuine democratic credentials - actively participated in the "Crusade for Freedom" conducted by the United States government in the early years of communist rule in Romania. However, as the period of "peaceful coexistence" began in the fifties and as American-Romanian relations improved in the 1960s, the aging members of the Committee became less active and less significant for its sponsors. In effect, the anti-communist opposition was voiced more systematically by Romanian employees of Radio Free Europe in Munich. Similar developments were noted also in England and France, where employees of the broadcasting media, dominated by Radio Free Europe, became the spokesmen for anti-communist, government-supported propaganda.

In the last analysis, however, all opposition, whether democratic or not, internal or external, could not threaten the communist dictatorship as long as the instruments of political control were unassailable. It did assume importance only after the collapse of the Ceausescu regime in December 1989 and in a manner unanticipated by those who believed that the fall of the communist dictatorship would lead immediately to the acceptance of western-style democracy.

Recent controversies regarding the character of the so-called "December Revolution" notwithstanding, it is evident that it was an internal Romanian phenomenon. Whether the Romanian army or the security police were more instrumental in insuring the success of the individuals who risked their lives in staging revolutionary actions in Timisoara, Bucharest, Cluj and other urban centers in December 1989 is still a matter of dispute. However, whether the "revolution" was in effect a "coup d'état" prepared by former communist leaders, with the knowledge and consent of military and security officers, which assumed the character of a revolution by the disgruntled and anti-Ceausescu masses is irrelevant to determination of the essential fact that the actions of December 1989 were a function of specific Romanian conditions and were planned and/or executed by Romanians.

The main goal of the participants in the "revolution" was to rid the country of the odious personal dictatorship of Nicolae Ceausescu and his wife, Elena Ceausescu. It was not a "democratic revolution" in the sense of seeking the transformation of the Romanian political order into a Dutch,

Danish, or American one. In other words, while the active participants in the revolution - students, industrial workers, intellectuals and other urban risk-takers - sought the restoration of basic human and civil rights, freedom of the press, religion, and assembly, the dissolution of the security police, the cleansing of the political apparatus, changes in economic and social policies, neither they nor the masses that hailed the fall of the Ceausescus were expressly concerned with party pluralism or free market economies. In fact, the vast majority of the advocates of democratic reform applauded the assumption of power by the so-called National Salvation Front, headed by Ion Iliescu and other anti-Ceausescu communists who were committed to the democratization of Romania.

Democratization, however, was to be a process that would take into account the specific conditions prevailing in Romania after twenty-five years of Ceausescu's dictatorship. And these "objective Romanian conditions" included the entrusting of the process of transition to democracy to a leadership with no experience in democratic governance, with limited knowledge of western democratic practices, and one vulnerable, because of its communist past, to attacks from the political emigration and its supporters at home and abroad.

The vulnerability of the Front's leadership was readily exploited by the external opposition which sought to regain power in post-Ceausescu Romania by discrediting it. Without exception, the leaders of the prewar historic parties, the National Liberal and National Peasant organizations, as well as those of the Iron Guard, denounced the National Salvation Front as communist and, in the case of the legionaries, also a Jewish-dominated, harborer of the Judeo-Bolshevik conspiracy that brought communism to Romania. Because of support of the anti-communist political emigration and identification of anti-communism with democracy, western governments, particularly that of the United States, ignored the political and economic realities facing the Front and made vitally needed economic assistance contingent on immediate implementation by the presumed communist-dominated Romanian government of democratic reforms and actions in the area of human and minority rights and on adoption of a market economy.

Armed with the weapon of their western supporters' withholding desperately needed economic aid by an impoverished but hopeful population, the external political opposition made inroads in Romania by co-opting anti-communist groups as well as by holding out the promise of western financial aid in the event that the communist-ridden Front were to be removed from power. These tactics proved to be less effective in discrediting the National Salvation Front in Romania than in Washington, London, and Paris. Whereas the moderate, democratically-oriented leaders of the National Peasant and National Liberal parties who returned from abroad focused on the democratic tradition of their organizations in the interwar years, on their anti-communism and the need for a new start, the political Right sought to secure the support of those segments of the population and pre-1989 officialdom that shared the common bond of nationalism, anti-Magyarism, anti-Russianism, and anti-Semitism.

Despite their efforts, the leaders of the historic parties who returned to Romania after 1989 had little success in securing support from the Romanian masses. This is because of they were regarded as outsiders who had not suffered under the Ceausescu dictatorship and did not participate in the "revolution" and also because of Ion Iliescu's popularity with the peasantry and working class. The nationalist Right, however, was able to co-opt the exponents and beneficiaries of Ceausescu's communist nationalism who could readily shift from the heathen nationalism of the Left to the Christian nationalism of the Right. In fact, the Right, unlike the pro-democratic parties, made Romanianism rather than democracy the criterion of political probity.

There can be little doubt about the Right's fomenting anti-Hungarian manifestations in Transylvania and violent demonstrations and actions of civil disobedience by sympathizers, or converts, directed against the "communist" and Jewish-infiltrated Front in 1990. The anti-Hungarian manifestations were blamed on the Iliescu regime by the political opposition but, more significantly, also by the United States and by the politically-active, irredentist and influential Hungarian diaspora in the United States who echoed the political line of the Hungarian government. Likewise, the forcible repression by the Front of violent anti-governmental demonstrations in Bucharest were interpreted by the opposition as well as by Washington and some of its allies as conclusive proof of the survival of communist attitudes and practices among the leaders of the National Salvation Front.

The ostracizing of Romania from the "democratic community," advocated and pursued energetically by the United States and some of its allies, mostly through withholding economic aid to the Romanian government while supporting actually or ostensibly "democratic" parties in Romania, did not prevent the election, and subsequent reelection, of Ion Iliescu as President of Romania or the retention of political control, in free parliamentary elections, by the renamed and revamped Democratic National Salvation Front. It did, however, lead to the adoption by the Romanian government of major economic reforms designed to expedite the transition to a genuine market economy and to insure Romania's eventual admission to the European Economic Community in the face of massive popular opposition to economic reforms which are leading to the pauperization of the population through rapid inflation, exorbitant prices, and below subsistence-level wages and pensions. On the other hand, the government has been reluctant to replace the entrenched bureaucracy or cleanse the military and police establishments of former "hard liners" or to contain the extremist nationalist propaganda spouted by the radical Right.

All things considered, democracy is alive, but not necessarily well, in post-communist Romania. The forms and requirements imposed by the western democracies are being met and implemented, albeit often à contre coeur, by the present regime. What is lacking, however, is a genuine commitment to democracy by the majority of the Romanian political organizations and the population at large. But that is not surprising since democracy, in practice and spirit, was never a paramount issue in Romanian political, socio-economic, and cultural life. It is not that the Romanian people are anti- or pro-democracy; rather, it is that democracy has been an essentially irrelevant concept in the history of a predominantly agricultural society or in the transition to an industrial one. The transformation of the agricultural society in the interwar years was hampered by the resistance to corresponding political changes by the dominant landed or expropriated aristocracy and to modernization and corollary socio-economic changes under the auspices of foreign, usually Jewish, urban capitalists by the nationalists of the Right. These adverse conditions for change, exacerbated by the global economic and corollary political crises of the 1930s, marked the end of the formal, anemic, democratic experiment of the interwar years to the benefit of anti-democratic, authoritarian, nationalist, xenophobic, anti-Semitic forces culminating in the totalitarian regime of Ion Antonescu and the Iron Guard.

There was little opposition to the dictatorship, little mass support for the continuation of the democratic experiment. There was much popular support for the goals enunciated by Ion Antonescu during the early years of the war - the recovery of the territories lost to foreign enemies in 1940 - but little for the anti-Semitic actions condoned by the dictatorial regime. There was continuing support for the anti-communist, nationalist policies of the short-lived "democratic" governments of the immediate post-Antonescu period. However, the extent to which democracy would have succeeded in post-World War II Romania, had it not been for the establishment of the totalitarian communist order, is difficult to determine. And it is still difficult to appraise the potential for democratic evolution of the isolated and largely despondent Romanian people in the post-Ceausescu years.

Inasmuch as the criteria for democratization formulated by the "western democracies" are largely incompatible with the historic evolution and political experience of both pre- and post-communist Romanian society, it may only be concluded that contemporary Romanian society is, generally, not anti-democratic. It is politically and ideologically anti-communist but not anti-statist. It is not against - in fact, it is largely in favor of - economic paternalism. It generally favors freedom of speech, assembly and of the press; it is for freedom of religion and is largely indifferent to active participation in party politics and to the activities of governmental institutions. In fact, it is not adverse to political paternalism. The majority of the population is not committed to the fulfillment of the nationalist historic legacy although it tends to be nationalistic. It is generally tolerant of minority rights as long as the minorities do not seek to secure special privileges at the expense of, or incompatible with, the interests of the majority.

Thus, while there is no necessary commitment, or even predisposition, to western democracy, there is general acceptance of the fundamental principles identified with such democracy. Nevertheless, under the adverse economic conditions attributable to the communist legacy and the callous indifference toward the country's needs displayed by most of the western democracies, it is likely, in the event of further deterioration of economic conditions, that a return to authoritarian, but not communist, rule would also be acceptable to the majority of Romania's population.